D0105228

# the welcome song

If you want to hear more of Jan Carlberg, here's how to contact her for speaking engagements:

*Write:*   Mrs. Jan Carlberg
        Gordon College
        255 Grapevine Road
        Wenham, MA 01984

*Tel.:* (978) 524-3709
*Fax:* (978) 524-3700
*E-mail:* jcarlberg@hope.gordonc.edu

To: Eleanor
May the peace & comfort of Christmas be with you and yours this
blessed time of the year.
Good health + joy in 2000

Love
Jan

1999

# the welcome song

### And Other Stories
### from a Place
### Called Home

## jan carlberg

**Fleming H. Revell**
A Division of Baker Book House Co
Grand Rapids, Michigan 49516

© 1999 by Jan Carlberg

Published by Fleming H. Revell
a division of Baker Book House Company
P.O. Box 6287, Grand Rapids, MI 49516-6287

Printed in the United States of America

**Library of Congress Cataloging-in-Publication Data**

Carlberg, Jan, 1940–
    The welcome song, and other stories from a place
called home / Jan Carlberg.
       p.  cm.
    ISBN 0-8007-1761-9
    1. Home—Religious aspects—Christianity. I. Title.
BR115.H56C37   1999
242—dc21                  98-48394

Unless otherwise indicated, Scripture quotations are from the HOLY BIBLE, NEW INTERNATIONAL VERSION®. NIV®. Copyright © 1973, 1978, 1984 by International Bible Society. Used by permission of Zondervan Publishing House. All rights reserved.

Scripture quotations marked KJV are from the King James Version of the Bible.

Scripture quotations marked NRSV are from the New Revised Standard Version of the Bible, copyright 1989 by the Division of Christian Education of the National Council of the Churches of Christ in the USA. Used by permission.

For current information about all releases from Baker Book House, visit our web site:

http://www.bakerbooks.com

To Jud,
for thirty-five years of faithfully doing your homework.
You built more than equity into a house.

Your godly life, serving heart, and disciplined ways
built us.

Thank you for modeling "a more excellent way"
without discouraging a struggler.

Your encouragement turned the spotlight on me
when you deserved star billing.

Mostly, thank you for demonstrating day after day to
our children and me, "There's no place like home."

# Contents

# Acknowledgments

To Mama for modeling the joys of home-making and for faithfully, joyfully carrying on after Daddy went home to be with the Lord. At eighty-two you continue to "stay fresh and green," proclaiming to the next generation that the Lord is your Rock (see Ps. 92:14–15).

To Heather Dawne, wise daughter, for pushing me to read wider and listen longer. Your model of discipline, perseverance, wit, compassion, creative hospitality, and contentment while studying for your M.D. challenges me. You first called me "Mama," growing my heart and our home.

To Chad Judson, thoughtful son, for pushing me to wrestle with words and think less like a "church lady." Your model of integrity, disciplined creativity, humor, love of family, and people skills encourages me. Your teachers were right: "You have potential." I'm blessed to be your mom.

To Matt Willis, son-in-love, for cheering me on and celebrating the idea of this book. You've infected our family with your *joie de vivre*. We seek no cure. Your model of loving Heather, family, friends, cycling, and life while balancing the demands of medical school amazes me.

To my small family of praying, loving friends: Carol Bussell, Gail MacDonald, and Joanna Mockler. Your model of friendship warms me. Your commitment to Christ informs me. Only God knows how little I'd accomplish without your secret support.

To the family we call Gordon College for allowing me the privilege of working with you at this place we've called home for twenty-two years. God's work among and through you excites me. This book and my life would be thinner without you.

To the trustees of Gordon College for choosing Jud and affirming me in the process by seeing us as a team. You draw the stories out of me. Sometimes you are the story through the generous giving of yourselves and your resources. You've blessed this place we've loved to call home.

To writers and thinkers, colleagues and friends: Sue Andringa, Diana Bennett, George and Darlene Brushaber, Jim Bultman, Sharon Eaton, Judy and Stan Gaede, Dave and Nancy Gyertson, Mary Eleanor Hurt, Marge Johnson, Jay and Janie Kessler, Ava Memmon, Steve Macchia, Judy Peterson, Mark Stevick, Lorna

Sawatsky, and Helene Winter, who pray, provoke, cheer, and/or convince me that I can weave a story from the interruptions and ordinary stuff of my life—even a trip to Dunkin' Donuts.

To Aunt Joyce and Uncle Howie for listening, laughing, and crying at appropriate places when I read some of these stories to you. Appreciative audiences aren't too easy to come by, especially from inside the family. You model such fun-loving, welcoming, home-cooked hospitality. I'll bet Jesus never fails to show up at your place. You give Russellville, Arkansas, a good name.

To Uncle Peter Stam for showing the rest of us what love looks like "for better or worse, in sickness and in health . . . 'til death parts us." Your love for Aunt Jeanelle set a new standard in our family. Thank you.

To Bill Petersen and Baker/Revell for giving me a second chance and a new publishing house to call home.

# Introduction

rowing up the eldest daughter of a Baptist preacher meant that, every Christmas, our family received a fair amount of "holy" gifts. Instead of a box of dark chocolates with nuts, or a puppy sporting a red bow, we tended to receive linen towel calendars or plaques with Bible verses or sermonettes. Our walls preached. Verses and sayings exhorted, challenged, rebuked, or taught wherever your eyes settled. "Home Sweet Home," "Prayer Changes Things," or "Jesus Christ the same, yesterday, today, and forever."

Annie Johnson Flint's poem "He Giveth More Grace" engraved on a plaque hung over Mama's kitchen sink. Years of washing and drying dishes slid that poem effortlessly into memory. A nearby wall proclaimed, "Jesus is the unseen guest at every table, the silent listener to every conversation." That alone should've kept us eating a good many of our meals in total silence. Yet, our family of five plus friends and relatives and whoever gathered 'round the table continued to express opinions, show emotions, speak truth, swap stories, or tell "knock-knock" jokes at the place we called home. But I never pictured Jesus eavesdropping, just listening, or laughing.

Home. So many images, feelings, memories. From way back drifts a picture of a scared first-grader running home for lunch and the safety of that place. It takes little to recall my months as a skinny six-year-old racing up the stairs to the back door of our second-floor flat in Chicago, yelling, "Mama, I'm home!"

At home I first learned the security of routines and boundaries. Mama taught the sacredness of ordinary tasks done well. Rituals moved the day along at a quieter pace. God seemed at home with order. Every noontime, while Mama fixed lunch, I listened to Aunt Teresa tell Bible stories from WMBI, the radio station of Chicago's Moody Bible Institute. One ordinary day, God used that ritual to get my attention. I met Jesus in my living room and asked Him to make my heart His home. He did with Mama sitting beside me on the floor. I met more than Mama, Daddy, or my brother Dan at our Fletcher Street flat. God showed up while I sat cross-legged in front of our big family radio that was shaped like a jukebox. A few days later, I walked the center aisle of the church I called home to "make my decision public" as Daddy urged.

Seventeen years later, I married and began hearing two of my favorite phrases—"Honey, I'm home" and (several years later) "Mom, I'm home." It didn't mean that some perfect world existed behind the closed doors of the places I've called home. But those places have been good schools for teaching and learning about love and life and God and His world. Two of my favorite subjects, Heather Dawne and Chad Judson, became my tough and much loved teachers. God saves children for some of His greatest work . . . true home schooling. Grandma and Mama called them "life's valuable lessons." Homework required.

For the past twenty-two years, Gordon College has become the place Jud and I and our children have loved to call home. Almost 1,500 students, plus faculty and staff, trustees, parents, friends, and alumni make for a big family. Some of the stories I share in this book come from this place and this community of people who share a common mission with Jud and me. And some come from my childhood home and from the home formed when Janice Dawn Jensen married R. Judson Carlberg.

One of the saddest words in our language is *homeless*. God intends for each of us to belong to someone, to be set in a family, to find sanctuary in a place called home. It doesn't always happen that way. But I believe God loves to show up in traffic, at hospital bedsides or in checkout lines, by office watercoolers or on park benches, giving us another chance to reconnect to His family, to belong. The heart of this book is incarnational . . . catching glimpses of a God who somehow loves us enough to show up, especially when we know we least deserve His company.

I hope these stories will encourage you to enjoy the journey and finish the race. So take another look at this Jesus and the ragtag bunch of followers He calls "family." It might help you imagine His plan to prepare a place for us, a forever home. A place where paint never peels, dust can't collect, taxes won't increase, and, best of all, the folks we love and trust never disappoint us. The Bible calls it heaven. We get to call it home.

*Part 1*

A Place to Believe

# Just like Ruth

*R*outine, aided by the alarm clock, shook me from my Monday morning sleep, nudging me to get up and fix breakfast for my family. Dark March mornings in New England encourage pulling the covers up and ducking under for a few extra minutes of sleep. So I hit the snooze button and curled up beside Jud for five minutes more.

Just enough consciousness took hold to set my mind in gear while my body rested. For starters: fix breakfast, dress, shove kids out the door to catch school bus, dishes, laundry, two phone calls . . . the daily duties before 9 A.M. Tomorrow I'd be teaching Joy Bible Study at Grace Chapel, my home church in Lexington, Massachusetts. I could hardly wait to get out of the kitchen and household chores and into the family room with my Bible and notebook. The logical place for God to show up.

We were studying women of the Bible. This week's subject was Ruth. While I rested, I tried picturing Ruth out in her barley field, doing her duty. My old Sunday school pictures showed her robed in blue, cradling a sheaf of grain, like some hoped-for baby. Reading the story more closely, I think she gathered the leftovers, not long stalks of barley. Stooping and snatching, then wiping back sweat and wispy strands of hair. Not a place for pretty hands or posturing about what might have been. I wonder what reflected back to Ruth from the mirror of her life?

The Bible's full of books bearing masculine names like Samuel, Isaiah, Joshua, Ezra, Job, and even Jonah. The newer testament includes John, Matthew, Peter, Luke, and more. Only a couple of women show up as book titles. Ruth's one. Makes me wonder about the place of hard choices and duty in God's scheme of holy work. God seemed to love to show up for Ruth, while she did her duty. No Bible or notebook in sight. I could use a visit.

The alarm interrupted my thoughts. After swatting it off, I swung my feet over the side of the bed and fished for my slippers. I caught hold of one and slipped my foot inside, then grabbed the other one. Pushing off from the bed, I stood on cushioned feet, calling the rest of me to attention. Morning waited.

As I shuffled from the bedroom through the hallway toward the kitchen, rehearsing the steps for making oatmeal, I caught my reflection in the mirror. It was just a blur. Nothing spectacular or worth a second glance. But I turned to face myself. I don't know why.

Before me stood a woman in her forties, dressed in a well-used flannel nightgown. This gown never heard of Victoria's Secret. Small bumps, typical flannel blemishes, peppered the gown, making it look slightly diseased. My hair stuck out like I'd been electrocuted but survived. The face looked like morning arrived ahead of schedule. A wave of depression washed over me. My eyes fixed on the mirror's image, freezing my slippered feet to the floor.

While I stood staring, my husband walked out of the bedroom. He stood behind me. Considerably taller than I, Jud wrapped his arms around me, rested his chin on the top of my head, and looked into that same full-length hall mirror. He neither laughed, moaned, nor keeled over at the choice he'd made some twenty years earlier. He simply squeezed harder, grinned, and said, "Trust me, honey. Don't believe everything you see."

I wonder if Ruth wore flannel.

# Mama Says, "Write!"

t's Labor Day. That's a holiday in Massachusetts where Jud and I live but not with Mama. I'd gone back home to North Carolina to write for a week. Mama managed telephone calls and alarm clocks so I could write or rest at appropriate times. This morning she woke the Westclox "rooster" that's plugged in beside her bed so I could sleep a while longer. I've got sensitive ears when it comes to bells, gongs, or roosters but sometimes struggle with quieter talk. That's a problem I have with God sometimes. He whispers. But not Mama. Her morning mercy lasted through breakfast; then, fortified with three cups of coffee and prayer, Mama strutted her Norwegian genes and ordered me out to her office to write.

So here I sit surrounded by photographs that tug me back in time, wall-mounted Bible verses that draw me to question if I have anything to say at all, and screen-door scenery that lures me back outside. The old ceiling fan stirs the hairs on my head and the ribbons on the basket beside the desk. They're empty of words—the basket and my head. Five years ago, that basket spilled over with cards and prayers for Mama while she fought cancer and we battled our worst fears.

"Write!" she shouts at regular intervals reminding me that God gave her the gift of advice. It's not listed as a spiritual gift, but don't tell Mama. "All bark; no bite," I remind myself while sitting and waiting on words.

"Write!" Mama barks from her kitchen control center. I hear and feel reverberations from her barking voice outside in the garage office where I'm twisting the hairs on my head and begging for a miracle.

Did Paul and Jeremiah sit and sweat like this? The prophet Jeremiah had more than his mother waiting on his words. Besides, he really did have the gift of advice. But nobody wanted to listen to him or to believe his words came from God. I don't understand a lot of what old Jer said to God's children, but when he said, "When your words came, I ate them; they were my joy and my heart's delight . . . ," I get it (Jer. 15:16). I'm sitting here starved for words.

How will I know if one or two of God's words show up? Do they come in King James language? Greek? Hebrew? Are they capitalized or in italics?

"It's awfully quiet out there!" Mama shouts. "Are you writing or sitting around waiting for a miracle?"

Now she's onto something. "A miracle sounds great!" I holler.

"You're it!" she snaps back.

I expect to be slapped on the back and start running to tag the next person. But just then God shows up like the enforcer of Mama's words. Suddenly the words "you're it" move from the safety of the ears under the hair I'd tangled to my heart where they settled.

"You're it!" Mama has been singing, praying, and shouting it for as long as I can remember. "You're the miracle, Janice Dawn." Mama doesn't mean it like some "feel good" pop psychologist or New Ager. She comes to conclusions through her sense of God's views; she finds them in the Bible.

Take Isaiah 41:13 for example: "For I am the LORD, your God, who takes hold of your right hand and says to you, Do not fear; I will help you." Mama believes God's words. She also believes that the words I seek aren't out there but in me where for some reason God lives. My heart, the place God loves to call home.

"Tink about it," my Norwegian bestemor (grandmother) would've said.

Gramma said, "Tink!"

Mama barks, "Write!"

So I "tink" I'll write until God or Mama say otherwise, or until I get the gift of advice.

# Picnic People

*A*s a Baptist preacher's kid, I grew up singing or hearing sung, "This world is not my home, I'm just a passing through." I heard sermons on setting my heart on "things above" and reminders that I was "a pilgrim on a journey." As our culture grew more materialistic, this world began to look more like my home through magazine photos, store windows, or television's best. Pilgrims, sojourners on life's journey, lived elsewhere. They popped into my pretty world through the evening news or photojournalism. They wore a lot of black. It's not hard to understand why they would choose to sing, "This world is not my home." A few plane crashes and bombings later, I find myself shuddering at this place I've called home and singing again, "This world is not my home, I'm just a passing through."

Pilgrims know about journeys and destinations but sometimes forget to picnic. Picnic people do both. They know their destination and commit to the disciplines of the journey, but the sounds of inextinguishable joy accompany them, and their love for the Lord of Life and all His creation motivates them to dare to picnic en route.

I'm a pilgrim on a journey to my true home. But I'd also love to be a picnic person.

Picnic people learn to travel light and share their loads. They check the skies for signs of storms so they're prepared. Troubles teach them to flex not fume. Picnic people expand their hearts and table to welcome prodigals and make the generations feel at home. Picnics provide natural settings for teaching truths without words. Picnics provide places for you to consider field lilies and sparrows and space to believe that nothing comes from worrying.

Surrounded by the stuff of this world and all its attractive distractions, we need a fresh crop of picnic people. We also need to connect with the long line of pilgrims who picnicked before us: Abraham and Sarah, Hannah, Joseph, Jacob and Rachel, Ruth and Naomi, Peter and Zacchaeus, Mary, and Martin Luther, John Wesley, Corrie ten Boom, and scores of men, women, and children who remain nameless until we all get *home* for the best picnic we could ever imagine.

We need a generation of men and women and children who declare "this world is not my home," not by retreating from it but by living in it like picnic people . . . pilgrims, sometimes tough and triumphant, other times stumbling and crawling but always heading together toward our true home.

The together part is both a wonderful and tough part of the journey. Even picnic people aren't all alike. God thought up diversity and "it was good." It seems to follow then that picnic people ought to be the best at gathering together all kinds and colors of people. Then, who knows, somebody might just hear us laughing or catch us hugging or smell the supper and ask if there's room for one more at the table. And God who thought up people and picnics will capture the scene for all eternity as one more person inches toward their true home. Lured by the laughter and love of a few faithful picnic people.

# Testimonies

*M*ama sat watching Scout, her Doberman. The dog stood neck stretched tall and hind legs extended in show dog style. "Isn't she beautiful and so sweet!" Mama exclaimed. I was hoping she was referring to me. Mama continued without a glance in my direction, "The Beezies say she's a champion. With her looks and lineage she could be a winner." After my feathers settled, I said, "Mama, you've got a new career ahead of you. You and Scout can hit the speaking circuit together." Mama laughed then shot back, "But that dog has no testimony."

Mama's right. Animals and angels have no testimonies, only people. I know the Bible talks about the heavens declaring the greatness of God (Ps. 19:1) and nature showing off God's wonders. But there's nothing like people for telling of God's love.

When I was much younger, testimonies were as regular as offerings in our Baptist church. Sunday evenings and Wednesday nights were incomplete without testimony time. There were always a few predictable people whose weekly word-for-word repetitions made it possible for any one of us kids to fill in should they ever have failed to show and tell. Whatever little space there was between the time the pastor opened it up to the congregation and the time of the first sharer was too much for these regular testifiers, so they filled it. Some folks don't do well with quiet.

But even a kid knew the real stuff. Those stories of people being saved. That's what we called it back then. Saved from what? From hell, for one thing. From themselves, for another. When they talked about Jesus and His love for them, you could actually begin to believe that this same Jesus loved you and would forgive your sins and give you a fresh start, if you asked Him. No wonder they still call it "Good News."

Some time ago at Gordon College, the place we call home, Tony Campolo preached on the topic of testimonies or titles. I can't remember it all, but the gist of the sermon went like this. Tony had attended an African American church on appreciation day, a time for recognizing graduates from high schools, colleges, and universities. The preacher praised them for their accomplishments and let them know that the world would be especially appreciative of their titles, but God cared about their testimonies. He warned them that one day they would die and people would gather 'round their graves, then head back to the church to eat potato salad and talk about them. His challenge was: "Do you want them to talk about your titles, or will you leave behind a testimony?" Tony built the story and concluded each level of the climb with: "Will you leave titles or testimonies?" By the end of the message, Gordon College students were cheering for testimonies.

Truth is, and truth's the heart of a testimony, not everybody favors them. Somewhere between when I was growing up and now, we've started favoring titles, even in the church. One problem with titles is that they can put distance between people. And some people confuse who they are with their titles. Testimonies tend to bring folks together, but not always.

A few thousand years ago, a man got into trouble for giving his testimony. The religious leaders, the Pharisees, preferred titles (theirs especially) or labels more than the gospel truth. The story's found in John 9 in the Bible. You see—well, that's the heart of the story—this man didn't see at all until God showed up. He'd been blind since birth. And that was his title or label—the blind man—until one extraordinary day when Jesus walked by and gave him a miracle.

I suppose he could've gotten by if he'd kept his mouth shut or played ignorant like his parents. But that's the thing about testimonies, at least the kind that grow from your own relationship with Jesus; you just can't keep quiet! My life's never been threatened for talking about Jesus. That worries me sometimes. I have often read about men and women and children who died because they wouldn't take back their testimonies; Jesus meant that much to them.

But Jesus meant nothing but trouble to the religious leaders. I don't think they minded the miracle nearly as much as they feared Jesus. So they did what scared folks often do; they took on somebody not their size. Remember how children have ways of making other kids change their stories or tell the truth? Maybe the Pharisees resorted to childish play and pounced on the man, pinning him to the ground with a demanding, "Take it back, blind boy!" But the man with the miracle eyes only blinked to distance himself from their hate; then he rose slowly, brushed the dirt from his clothes, and spoke so even a child could understand. "This one thing I know. I once was blind but now I see."

The religious leaders must have squinted, then shaken and badgered their eyewitness about the particulars of his testimony. But the man with the startled eyes wasn't complaining about Who healed him or how or when it was done. He was too busy taking in his mama's face for the first time and watching the dog who'd guarded his begged-for coins cock his head and hook a good gaze into his master's still surprised-looking eyes.

Later on, after the religious leaders kicked that little truthteller out of the church, Jesus found him and took him into His confidence. He asked the man with the thankful eyes, "Do you believe in the Messiah?" and the man said, "Who is He? I want to."

And Jesus said, "You have seen Him, and He is speaking to you!" And next thing you know, this ordinary-nobody-special-kind-of guy's taking a good, long look into the face of Jesus, the long-hoped-for Messiah, and stating the beginning of his testimony, "I believe."

Those Pharisees can keep their titles. I'd rather have a testimony, a true story about Jesus and me. Mama's dog, Scout, won't ever be able to give one, nor will angels or that blind beggar's dog, if he had one. They'll never get to experience or tell about God's grace and mercy. But you and I, we're another story in the making, if we aren't too blind to see when God shows up to offer us a miracle. Sometimes, right in the middle of the place we love to call home.

# The Recipe

od liked Grandma's kitchen. I don't really have any theological basis for saying that. It's just that God seemed to show up there pretty regularly, especially at suppertime. Bestemor (that's Norwegian for grandmother) never made the cover of *Gourmet* or *Bon Appetit* magazines. But she could cook. And she did it without a recipe card or cookbook in sight. Grandma cooked from scratch, the old-fashioned way.

"Grandma, I'd love to have your recipe for chocolate cake," I pleaded one day.

And she replied, "Oh, ve yust need some cocoa and a few tings to make dat. It's easy."

We defined *easy* differently.

God never actually sat at my grandparents' table as far as I know. But early on we knew that "Jesus is the unseen guest at every table, the silent listener to every conversation." It was written on the wall. God was not a negative force glaring across the table until the last vegetable disappeared. He laughed through Grandma's eyes and served big slices of lemon meringue pie through her hands. He spoke wonderful words of life through her mouth. "No, Yanice; Papa vill help me dry da dishes. Tank you for asking."

Grandma never read Erma Bombeck. I did. Erma died some time ago. Sometimes she made me think of Bestemor. Erma had a way of slipping truth in through a story. This was Grandma's style. We used to read Erma in the *Boston Globe*, but some editor scratched her column, leaving Massachusetts and me in need of some laughs.

Grandma'd already been in heaven for more than ten years when Erma wrote this in her newspaper column, *At Wit's End*. Someone had written in, complaining that her mother washed aluminum foil and plastic bags and found ways to use even chicken necks. Erma responded, "I think I know your mother . . . she's a lot like mine . . . and a whole generation who lived through the Great Depression. She has learned what she must have for real life, and she has learned what she can live without. Knowing that makes all the difference."

That's partly why I think God liked Grandma's kitchen. Grandma knew what she needed for real life. And God knew He topped her short list. So they joined forces. Well, Grandma's weakness linked up with God's strength to form that force. Limited resources coupled with total trust in God made miracles their forte. God seemed to love to stretch her soup to feed shut-ins and to multiply her meatballs like manna. Amazing "tings" happened when God and Grandma wore aprons. I can hear her now: "Vell, it vill be interesting to see how God vorks dis vun out."

Often I puzzled over God's ways. As two second-generation preachers' kids, my husband, Jud, and I knew hospitality was not optional at the place we loved to call home. But neither was our tight budget, so what was I to do? Call in the pros—Mama and Grandma. Tested experts. Each passed on inspired tips for multiplying loaves and fishes and chocolate chip cookies, a recent addition to the staff of life. But one of Grandma's recipes grew my heart, not my hips. That's partly why I had to get to Brooklyn back in 1965.

We did. Jud and I took off for Brooklyn to gather with family and friends to celebrate Grandma and Grandpa Tweten's fiftieth wedding anniversary. We were newlyweds living in Denver, where Jud was a middler at Denver Seminary. Grandma and Grandpa, after pastorates and ministries in Canada, Wisconsin, Illinois, and New York were back in Brooklyn. There they stood, smiling like newlyweds and sharing their recipes for lasting love.

Grandpa beamed, "Ya, in all da world, dere is no vun like Mama."

And Grandma shocked us with, "And, Papa, you've been a good, faithful lover." Until then, we'd never grasped that they too used the since-the-world-began method for conceiving children.

The day after the celebration, I sat alone with Bestemor in her kitchen. "Grandma, I need some help," I said. She looked relieved that I'd come. "I need some of your recipes, especially cheap ones that can feed a lot of people."

"Ya, Yanice. I know a lot about sheap recipes."

"Since you mentioned sheep, how about your lamb stew? It always stretched like old elastic."

"Ya, dat vun is special. Dere's a secret to it. Get your paper and pencil, and I vill tell you."

While I rooted in my purse for a scrap of paper or an index card, Grandma simply sat, hands folded in her aproned lap. Tools in hand, I begged her to begin.

Grandma's eyes twinkled as she spoke. "Da secret to my lamb stew is no lamb."

Now understand me, Grandma cooked well and prepared nourishing and tasty meals. But her frugality grew out of necessity not a personality disorder. So I waited a few seconds before probing.

"Bestemor, how much lamb per stew?"

"Like I said. Dere is no lamb in my stew."

While my jaw dropped, hers spread into a wide grin, then sprung open and spilled out a laugh. I wrote "try her meatballs" in the margin of the recipe.

"Ya, I'm telling da trut. Ve didn't have da money for da lamb. I vould go to da butcher and ask for a mutton bone vit a liddle meat maybe. Den I vould take it home and put it in a kettle of vater vit seasonings. I vould cook it and cook it and den add da potatoes, onions, and carrots. And last I vould ticken it vit flour and serve it in von of my fancy dishes. Do you know how to ticken tings, Yanice?"

"Yes, Grandma. I can 'ticken tings.'"

Grandma responded with, "Do you tink I still have an accent?"

"Yust a liddle vun," I said, scanning the ingredients. The recipe looked as sparse as her budget and mine: Get lamb bones, add water, toss in some roots and a few seasonings, and "ticken it." The real trick would be trying to stay "tankful" while playing Old Mother Hubbard.

"Grandma, is that all there is to the stew?"

"No, Yanice. Yust listen and write. If I have some fresh parsley, I sprinkle some on top."

That "IF you have some . . ." trait separated the sheep from the "no lambs." It divided an older generation from mine. If we didn't have it, we worked overtime to get it. Contentment and materialism are oxymorons.

"Next," Grandma rose from her chair, folded her hands under her chin, and looked toward the heavens from whence cameth her help, "I pray over it, Yanice, and den bring da lamb stew to da table and pass it around."

I sat stunned, then blurted out, "Grandma, all those years I thought everybody else got the lamb before it got to me."

Grandma laughed. "Vat do you tink I vas praying for in da kitchen!" Then she added, "Yanice, you live in a vorld ven people tell you dat you must have lamb in your stew to be happy and you better have extra in your freezer too. I lived a good life vitout any lamb in my stew for vun good reason. I know da Lamb of God, and He knows and loves me."

Too many years and stews separate me from Grandma and that tiny kitchen where God worked wonders. I like imagining God and Grandma in aprons, stirring up the stuff we can't live without. Grandma's too much of a Lamb lover for God not to show up, even on a recipe card. My biggest problem's been where to store the recipe. I know to file it under "L" but can't decide between "lamb stew" or "life's valuable lesson."

# Faith to Fish or Fly

*L*ast week, the presidents and spouses from the Christian College Consortium gathered at Billy Graham's training center, The Cove, near Asheville, North Carolina. Spring shows up early or on time in those parts. Forsythia, azaleas, daffodils, jonquils, tulips, redbuds, dogwoods, willows, and weeping cherries strutted their stuff. Sneezing's a small price to pay for God's spring palette.

A free Saturday afternoon gave a niche of time to wind down to Tryon, North Carolina, to visit old friends Nate and Jewel Hubley. It's good to spend time with longtime followers of Jesus. Our conversations weren't clogged with yesterdays and might-have-beens. Eyes connected, ears perked up to catch the latest news about Gordon College, the place we love to call home.

Walking the halls, touring the life care facility where the Hubleys now live, gave insights into these seasoned disciples, experienced fisherfolks. They know most fish by name. Nate's started a Bible study. They're involved at their church, teaching Sunday school. None of this, "It's somebody else's turn now." They're fishing in fresh waters with nothing but keepers in sight; the lures of tested faith in God, a thankful heart, and joy for the journey catch fish.

On the way back to Asheville, I asked Jud to stop in Hendersonville, the heart of apple country, for a gander and meander through this quaint southern town. Jud put his seat back for a twenty-minute nap while I took in the four blocks of a simpler life. As I headed back toward the car, I nearly tripped over a slouched sermon illustration. The old man's left leg stretched across too much of the sidewalk while his other leg folded under him, forming a true laptop on which to balance his painting.

I wouldn't have glanced again except for the young girl who stopped and applauded his creation with, "Wow, mister. That's real good." His appearance told that he'd been coloring outside the lines for a long time. At quick glance the canvas looked plopped with browns and whites, like a rest stop for birds flying south. The white-blobbed brush hovered just above the canvas while he debated where to land. His unsteady hand struggled to settle while the glob of white paint aired 'til it could do neither much good nor harm.

As I inched closer, I noticed fine blue lines, small numbers, and the shape of an eagle, wings spread for soaring. The wannabe artist seemed stuck on the brown and white blobs of the painting, perhaps not unlike his life. God's truth stuck in me like wadded cotton. Where were Nate and Jewel when I needed them? They'd know how to fish or cut bait. I only hooked his eyes, then slipped off to our car, leaving the unfinished masterpiece sitting on the bench holding his attempt at real life.

Yesterday I hurried to the art gallery at Jenk's to see George Wingate's "Containers" exhibit. I slipped in while George was taking down his collection. My favorite was George's address book. It contained friends. It's good to get back to this place I love to call home, a place where people paint without numbers. But I don't want to get so comfortable that I forget how to fish like Nate and Jewel or how to connect with God's much-loved containers, sitting on benches or sleeping on sidewalks, struggling to paint an eagle by numbers when they were meant to soar like one.

# Weather Forecasts and Other Myths

eather forecasters have a way of kicking sand in my face. All week they've pelted me with threats about Friday. Not the hope-filled style of Tony Campolo ("It's Friday, but Sunday's coming!") but a pessimistic countdown 'til cloudbursts. Catching their predictions is a form of reeling in a daily dread.

Tomorrow's the Friday they've fussed about all week. We're due to be slapped with a "major" storm. The college trustees are meeting. Some are bringing their children to check out "our" college. We need sunshine and smiles, the way it looks on all those catalogues and brochures we mail to prospective students. This is the time to strut not slosh! Only L. L. Bean models look cool in duck boots. So I pray my New England SOS, "Send it out to sea, Lord."

It's Sunday now. Trustees, their kids, my SOS prayer, and the storm came and went. Except for some clouds, debris, and soggy shoes, you'd never know we'd been broadsided with a nor'easter. Faculty, staff, trustees, planning committees worked 'til the Son did shine . . . a fitting footnote to Genesis week, a special chapel series to launch the beginning of fall semester.

Dr. Charles Price, guest speaker for Genesis week and our interim dean of the chapel, urged us to take off our shoes. Like Moses, we needed to give God our shoes so we would walk in His ways. Not pretty paths, usually. For most of us, the same shoes we offered up to God to fill and walk in on Wednesday were the soggy ones we sloshed about in on Friday.

Which is pretty much life at Gordon College or any place we choose to call home. Most of the time we make commitments in sandals and sunshine then find that life's more like duck boots and downpours. Well, no matter what's on your feet, they're beautiful. Check out Isaiah 52:7 and celebrate the God who shows up in sandals or duck boots. Oh, and work and live each day like you believe "Sunday's comin'." What does channel 5 know about real life anyhow!

# Plane Talk

*M*ama sat watching a fleet of yellow butterflies land and take off from her garden's field. I kept trying to read yesterday's news, while Mama gave forth on another world.

"Look at them, Janice."

I glanced up, gave them a rolling eye, then dove back into the paper.

"Do they have a leader?" She'd interrupted my scanning of world news.

"Who?"

"The butterflies!"

"I don't know," I mumbled.

Mama went right on. "Well, it's a pretty amazing sight. Hundreds of yellow butterflies showing up right on schedule."

Anything on schedule amazes me as I head out to Mama's office, an hour behind, to write. Her desk sits just a few feet from the screen door. It's a perfect spot for thinking and writing. But today I'm viewing fresh recruits, batches of butterflies, flying in to do their work. "Right on schedule," as Mama would say.

Mama stood on the porch outside the office screen door and interrupted with, "I wonder how long those butterflies flew to get here?"

"Mama, I don't have time to wonder."

She smiled sad-like and headed into the garden.

Sometimes my work requires flying. Just two days ago, I flew across the country to attend my cousin's funeral. That's work, even though U.S. Air bumped me up to first class. A nonstop coast-to-coast flight takes the better part of a day and most of my strength.

When I travel, I often bring too much work and not enough wonder. This time, I packed the computer and some of my Norwegian genetic hard drive. A little stiff body language usually gives me the freedom to avoid unwanted conversations. The man seated next to me stiffened and dodged eye contact as both of us switched on our computers.

Flying first class presents some challenges along with the perks. Attendants keep interrupting with food, drinks, free movies, and in-flight entertainment. I don't mean like dancers or clowns coming down the aisles, at least not paid ones.

After the flight attendant cleared away our meals, we resumed our work. Every now and then I glanced at his screen displaying facts, figures, charts, and graphs. I wondered if he read my work when my head was down. Did he pick up on the name of "Jesus" every now and then? I wondered if he read enough to know that I'm a Christ follower or just enough to think he caught me swearing.

The pilot interrupted my thoughts with the announcement of upcoming sights. Next his guided tour began. It's happened to me before. Once in a while you even get a pilot with a sense of humor. A couple of years ago when I was flying from Boston to California, the pilot interrupted with, "If you'll look to your right, you'll see the Hoover Dam, named for a famous vacuum cleaner." Most acted like they weren't listening; a few snickered, but I laughed out loud. Mostly because the passenger in front of me blurted, "I never knew that!"

There's a lot I've learned while flying. One fact is that whatever side the scenery's on, I'll be seated on the other. Today was no exception. I was 4F, and the view belonged to the ABC side of this jet. It takes effort not to read too much into my 4F status.

The pilot instructed passengers on the left side of the plane to look out and see a "magnificent view of Yosemite." From the right side I saw some trees. I was beginning to feel like Charlie Brown trick or treating and finding rocks in his sack. I never saw the Hoover Dam either.

There's a story in John 6 about Jesus, His disciples, and a crowd of folks who found themselves on the wrong side of each other. The day before, Jesus fed this crowd of more than five thousand with a boy's lunch and a miracle. When they realized that Jesus and His disciples were on the other side of the lake, they got into boats and crossed over to find Him.

Once they saw Jesus, they asked, "Rabbi, when did you get here?" (v. 25).

Now that qualifies as small talk.

But Jesus headed straight for their hearts and answered,

> "I tell you the truth, you are looking for me, not because you saw miraculous signs but because you ate the loaves and had your fill. Do not work for food that spoils, but for food that endures to eternal life, which the Son of Man will give you. On him God the Father has placed his seal of approval."
>
> Then they asked him, "What must we do to do the works God requires?"
>
> Jesus answered, "The work of God is this: to believe in the one he has sent."

verses 26–29

But most didn't believe, not even when God showed up in Jesus. So they demanded more miracles, grumbled, argued, and questioned this God in disguise. And after exhausting themselves with finger pointing, beard pulling, eyebrow raising, and tongue wagging, most of them made a choice. They settled for "so what," and from then on, "many of his disciples turned back and no longer followed him" (v. 66), since this teaching was too hard. All but one of the twelve disciples stayed with this God in sandals, but most everybody else distanced themselves from Jesus and cast their vote for the other side.

Jesus disappointed many. The crowds felt He never did enough miracles. Too many suffered and died for one thing, and He didn't fit their thoughts of God for another. And some still choose to come down on the opposite side of Jesus because of ongoing suffering and evil and wrong notions of God. I understand some of that anguish. We prayed for my cousin Douglas yet he died. No miracle stopped the cancer from consuming his vital organs.

But a miracle did keep Douglas from ending up on the wrong side. You see, the One who made the butterflies and sent them off to work on schedule, that same God made Douglas. And when my cousin was young and living in Arkansas, God showed up in his Grandma Jensen and in a little Baptist church where Dougie asked Jesus to be at home in his heart.

And so we gathered by a lake for Doug's memorial service, like people gathered two thousand years ago when God wore sandals. Not all believed then or now. But that didn't keep God from showing up. That's why I couldn't help but sing Doug's testimony. So I shut my eyes and flew back to when we were kids and sang, "Jesus loves me. This I know, for the Bible tells me so." There's a miracle tucked inside that song for people of all ages, the kind we need more than health or wealth. Doug's body's back to dust, but he lives with Jesus and family and friends who chose on earth to believe that Jesus is Who He says He is and did what He said He did. The Bible tells us so.

Mama's right. It's good to wonder. All work and no wonder may just put you on the side with the crowds who thought Jesus taught too tough, and so they left. Being seated on the 4F side of the plane made me miss some sights. It's one thing to miss Yosemite. It's another to miss the One who made it all and has a scheduled departure for more than just butterflies.

# Knee Deep in Renewal

ast week while the campus paused for a Day of Prayer, I sampled springtime in North Carolina on a quick trip to see my mom. She needed encouragement and I needed spring.

We slept late and took naps like pooped people should—Mom recovering from flu and I from flying. It happened the second morning of my four-day visit. I awoke early by habit so planned to go for a walk while Mom slept. En route to the bathroom, I decided to hurdle the gate planted to keep the dog from roaming the house. Somewhere between taking off from the kitchen and landing in the breakfast nook, my nightgown altered a simple flight plan. The gown drooped just enough to hook the gate as I flew too low, which sent me crashing, taking a rug-burning slide across the breakfast room and slamming my knees into the bathroom door. As a baseball fan, I longed to hear, "Safe!" All I heard was a dog's whimper.

Oddly enough my first reaction was to see if anyone was looking. Whew! Only one terrified dog, Scout, sat wide-eyed near the downed fence. You've got to work to scare a Doberman. Mama slept. I moaned and Scout nuzzled my face. Trust me, you don't want to visualize this scene.

I pictured Gordon's campus at prayer on bended knees while I used mine for lower purposes. It didn't help to hear my mind singing, "Pass me not, O gentle Savior, hear my humble cry! While on others Thou art calling, do not pass me by." Nor did it comfort me to recall that my God knew when I sat, stood, or fell because He neither slumbered nor slept. With my gown higher than my thoughts, I could only hope He napped or dozed.

Later, while eating breakfast, Mama asked me what I'd like her to leave me when she dies. I said, after such a humble beginning to my day, "that clothesline post." She laughed but questioned neither my wish nor my sanity. You see, that post and I go way back. In the years before Jud and I gave Mother and Daddy a clothes dryer, it was one of two posts supporting two metal lines from which all sheets, towels, and underwear dripped until dry. After the dryer, mostly swimsuits and beach towels hung from those lines. But in recent years, tall grandchildren risked decapitation as they ran after frisbees and other flying objects, so the rusty wires came down. Now all that remained of our pre-industrial revolution were two posts: one sporting a birdhouse and the other, my inheritance.

My post stood like Aaron's rod, sprouting life out its top. It was Psalm 1:3—"like a tree planted by streams of water, which yields its fruit in season" and Psalm 92:12, 14—"The righteous will flourish like a palm tree . . . they will still bear fruit in old age, they will stay fresh and green." Any survivor of winter seeks samples of spring. Which is why I love that post with a wee tree peeking out its top, green and growing, full of hope. It's like God showed up full of springtime renewal. Enough to break out in posts or people.

Mom and my knees are better now, and a sample of southern spring can last 'til winter backs down in New England, the place I love to call home. A bloomin' post is a great inheritance, but I'd recommend a shorter nightgown or a lower gate for first-time hurdlers. Renewal's meant to be an inside job.

*Part 2*

A Place of Hope

# Wigglers Welcome

*N*obody'd call it church. After all, it was Saturday, and the crowds lined up were planning on a few hours at one of New England's best craft fairs. I handed over my coupon for a one-dollar discount and paid the remaining four-dollar admission fee. Small price for such a grand display of creativity. A warehouse in Woburn is not the kind of place where you'd expect God to show up.

The pack of people moved as one down the center aisle. I strained to see some gettin' off place when I spotted a sign above me on the right. It read, "Wigglers Welcome." I twisted free from the mob and squished into the small space. The artist's booth housed one smiler with scissors, one wiggler, and one anxious mom. Looking like patience perched on a stool, the gray-haired craftswoman snipped away at a piece of black paper until she'd birthed another silhouette. All three seemed pleased with the result: one wiggler captured like still life. Amazing.

Kids came, most forced, some crying and struggling to get free. Most remained corralled until captured by a twinkly eyed artist with a love for wigglers. The kids caught it, a love more tangible than the snipped rendering of themselves. The artist drew them in with those eyes and a laugh ready to spill out and bless the children and the moms who brought them. Both needed a blessing more than a reminder to sit still or relax. Seems like God showed up to laugh and bless the artist and any of us onlookers.

Later, at the grocery store, I watched wee wigglers getting plopped into carts, a few spanked for their curiosity. I watched older wigglers switching lanes, trying for the fastest route out. They're easy to spot when you're one of them. Judging by some of the looks, most folks don't care much for wigglers.

As one of those older wigglers, I take hope from people like Zacchaeus, Peter, Sarah, and Rebekah. They weren't good at sitting still or coloring within the lines either. Zach wiggled up a tree, Peter wiggled out of ever having known Jesus, Sarah wiggled Hagar into Abe's arms, and Rebekah wiggled the blessing for Jacob out of Isaac. But not one of 'em wiggled fast or far enough to twist away from God's loving reach. Like that seasoned artist, He just kept smiling and snipping away until a silhouette emerged bearing the resemblance of Someone greater than we'd ever catch in a mirror.

Church leaders might do well to take a second look at craft fairs as the next site for teacher training or community outreach or evangelism. We might do better at taking some of the quotes and hard to decipher verses off those outdoor church bulletin boards and replacing them with a simple message, "Wigglers welcome." Can't hurt, and it could just draw a few more folks in to sit still a while. Hopefully, they'd sit long enough for God, the Master Artist, to begin snipping away while telling them a story about His grand purpose for them and how He'd welcome their invitation to let their hearts become the place He would just love to call home.

# Not Just Any Old Name

od showed up yesterday on my drive from Breckenridge to Frisco, Colorado. It's less than ten miles but enough time for God to get my attention. This time He wrote it across several mountain peaks.

Even though it was near the end of July, snow still topped some peaks, outlined others, and hid in crevices like long drips of frosting. Suddenly something caught my eye. The way the snow outlined or dripped up and down this range seemed to spell something. I looked closer and saw clearly one word, *NAME*. The *E* seemed a little blurred, but the rest appeared as clear as God's mountain tablet.

There was no place to pull over, so I continued toward Frisco, puzzling over God's short note to me and any who chose to look up. Made me think about the bright graffiti I'd seen on water towers, highway under-passes, and wherever young lovers, recent high school grads, or gangs chose to leave their mark. God's graffiti hurt no one, defaced nothing, and said something worth remembering.

That word took me back to the wee hours of one day last winter. I say "day" only because it was about three A.M. when my husband woke me to say, "Do you know you are crying in your sleep?" I didn't. Jud slipped his arms around me and said, "You were talking to Jesus and calling out the names of the children. Let's pray and turn this over to God." Jud prayed, then turned over and fell asleep.

How could he just turn it over to God and sleep? I needed to do my part: weep, worry, and wrestle with God. But only when no one was looking, or I'd get no extra credit. Not that I actually said or consciously thought this, but when I look back, my behavior revealed what I really believed.

I wrestled my pillow from under my head and pushed it onto my face. College presidents need their few hours of sleep, and I didn't want to interrupt Jud again with my fears and tears. So I sobbed into my pillow until exhaustion took over.

In the quiet that followed, God whispered, "Jan, what is My name?" This is not a tough question for a second-generation Baptist preacher's kid. I wiped my sore nose with a wet tissue and whimpered, "Jesus." I always think of Jesus when I'm flattened by something or someone.

Nothing. No buzzer or gong hinting that I'd given a wrong answer. No applause either. Just more nothing. The kind of quiet when you sense something major's about to happen. I clammed up so I wouldn't miss anything.

Such stillness dried my eyes and nose and set my senses at full attention. Finally that still voice asked again, "What is My name?"

No longer on automatic pilot, like someone answering a Sunday school quiz, I waited and puzzled. Suddenly, like a computer just plugged in, my memory drew up a verse learned long ago. The verse God used to instruct rose to my consciousness, nudged up by His Spirit within me.

Many years earlier, in the place I first called home, Daddy had worked with me to help me learn this Bible verse for a Christmas pageant. I felt proud learning such a big verse as a small child. "For unto us a child is born, unto us a son is given: and the government shall be upon his shoulder: and his *name* shall be called Wonderful, Counsellor, The mighty God, The everlasting Father, The Prince of Peace" (Isa. 9:6 KJV, italics mine).

Suddenly, like the psalmist David, hundreds of years before me, I sat up, ready for school "in the watches of the night" (Ps. 63:6 NRSV), with God as my teacher.

After some awful quiet, I answered, "Wonderful Counselor." Instantly God's Spirit washed me with fresh awareness of what it meant for me, my kids, nieces and nephews, cousins' kids, friends' children, and Gordon College students for whom I cried and prayed. I and they have a "Wonderful Counselor."

Into my dark night shot the light of perspective. This Wonderful Counselor could listen and counsel them in their beds, while they slept with resistance down. He could sit by them in libraries, beside desks, at exam time, in cars on dates, at work when stressed. Wherever they were, He already was. No appointment necessary. No cash or insurance coverage required. I cried with hope and relief, "Oh, Wonderful Counselor, I trust You to customize Your counsel for each of these kids. Thank You for reminding me of Your name."

As I rolled over to go to sleep, having learned my lesson, I heard, "What is My name?" Nothing followed. Then I heard myself shout, "Mighty God!" How Jud slept through that, only God knows. Such strong truth lifted my spirits. This Mighty God saves, heals, and forgives. This Mighty God flings stars into place, sculpts mountains, gouges seas and riverbeds. This Mighty God puts kings and governments into place and pulls them down at His will. This Mighty God thought up and formed people in His own image. He can tend these young men and women I remind Him of in the wee hours of the morning. "I get it. I get it. It's not on me; it's on You!" I shout.

Catching on to God's pattern, I wait and stare into the dark around me until I hear, "Jan, what is My name?" The awesomeness of the moment shushes me. To think that I'm in school and God's teaching me! Running the verse through my mind, I come to "Everlasting Father." Having loved my daddy so much, it's easy for me to conceptualize "Father." Not that my dad did it all right; he made some major mistakes, especially at the halfway point of the race. So I puzzled about the "everlasting" part of God's name.

Plenty of college students and some from within our larger circle of family and friends have "never-ready dads." They broke promises, showed up late or seldom, mocked marriage, climbed ladders, and accumulated stuff instead of being everlasting, truth-telling dads. Moms aren't off the hook in this culture either. So I find myself praying, "Everlasting Father, be to each child the parent they most need. Let Your unconditional love underscore their worth. You with the Name above all names, let them choose their identity in You. Teach them promise-keeping, truth-telling, time-valuing, money-managing, and relationship-building."

By now I could hardly wait for God's final question. When I heard, "What is My name?" I nestled close to this God above all gods and breathed, "Prince of Peace." The contrast between the chaos and complexity of our culture and anything peaceful amazes me. "Dear Prince of Peace, bring order out of their chaos. Help them simplify the complexities of their world. Out of the cacophony in and around them, let them pick out Your still small voice. I rest in You, Powerful and Sweet Prince of Peace."

And I did rest. And still do rest in the reminders of His names. When the enemy slithers up to whisper fear in my ears, sometimes I start back down into the pit with him. But before long, I remember and call on the names of the Lord: Wonderful Counselor, Mighty God, Everlasting Father, and Prince of Peace.

I thought Jud slept because he didn't get it. He didn't know the potential for danger or care as much as I. So he just quietly called on the name of the Lord, prayed a simple prayer, rolled over, and slept like a baby. Now I suspect Jud knew a few more of God's names. Best of all, there's more. Look 'em up the next time you're tempted to weep or wimp out from calling on just any old name when only God will do.

# Dream Aisles

*F*inancial pages, stock prices, business closings, and mergers don't interest me much; the price of green grapes usually grabs my attention. But yesterday's newspaper brought word on the front and financial pages that Woolworth's is closing their stores in this country. It seems that the K-marts and Wal-marts squeezed the old giant of the five-and-dime stores until all it could do was throw up its hands and shut its doors. I feel sad. It was more than a store to me.

When I was a child, Woolworth's stocked dreams. Where else could I go with no money in my pockets and watch exotic birds up close—parakeets spitting seeds, canaries cocking heads and singing to a penniless dreamer. A kid like me touched turtles, watched hamsters at work, then chased goldfish with that long-handled net when no clerk hovered nearby. I didn't feel poor because I couldn't buy them but rich because they were within reach of my senses. For me, that was the "scent" part of the five- and ten-cent store.

Sometimes Mama and I ventured to town to take in the windows of our few stores. No interior decorating genius dressed Woolworth's windows. It seemed like some fun-loving kid had stuffed those glass boxes with dreams. Depending on the season, you'd find yo-yos and baby chicks, bicycles and beach balls, pencils and plaid flannel shirts, or sleds, skates, and shovels. Dish towels, scrub buckets, and spools of colored thread lured Mama up and down those oiled wooden floors. Paper dolls and coloring books drew me to my aisle of dreams.

Back-to-school season sent Daddy and me treasure hunting at Woolworth's. Tablets and pencils made up the list. No need for lunch boxes since I walked home for lunch. I remember showing Daddy the latest crayons, sixteen in a box, and hinting how I'd love to have some new ones for Christmas. Times must've been extra good, because they showed up with my new tablet and pencils for the first day of school. Daddy loved delivering dreams.

Sometime in mid-December, while my brothers napped and Mama baked, Daddy and I pulled on our boots and tramped to town for an afternoon of serious shopping. Slippin' my mittened hand into his leather glove felt like hookin' up with Santa. Sometimes we'd run and slide like crazy kids, making the journey as fun as getting there.

Once inside, we "whewed" the sights of Woolworth's. Mama always gave Daddy a list. I'd watch him tuck it dutifully into his pocket then forget it while he played Santa Claus for one small afternoon. He never forgot Mama's needs. It's just that simple stuff's remembered easily. Four red candles, one spool of "the cheapest" wrapping paper, one box of tinsel, a little hard candy, and maybe a package of paper napkins with poinsettias on them made up Mama's wish list. It's fun to shop for somebody who has little and wants even less.

Aisles piled high as jungle grass became our hunting ground. Daddy and I combed the counters for Tinker-toys for my brother Danny, wooden blocks for Ralph. I splurged on Mama with a new dish towel and a bottle of Evening in Paris perfume in a midnight blue bottle. Aunt Harriet usually gave me her old bottles, great for playing dress-up. A little water brought that exotic scent to life. Daddy usually got Tweed perfume for Mama at the drugstore; that soared out of my price range. Mama and I would come the next week to buy Daddy ink for his Parker pen and some new socks and handkerchiefs. It was hard to imagine anyone richer than we or a place more wondrous than Woolworth's.

My kids grew up with K-mart and Toys-R-Us and places too overstocked and stimulated to leave much room for dreaming. Sales clerks in matching tops or T-shirts never quite measured up to the mix of folks who answered questions, blew up balloons, and tended you like family. Sometimes odd, but family-like nonetheless.

I know. I *was* one when I turned fourteen. My first real job with a paycheck came from a five-and-dime store just outside of Atlanta, Georgia. My area displayed towels, sheets, and fancy dresser scarves and doilies. Most of my first few paychecks went to spring a huge striped beach towel from the layaway department. This serious towel gave more to hide behind when we changed clothes at the lake. When you're fourteen, privacy's worth a price.

The towel's thin as gauze now. But I've kept it to remind me of my rich past. While I was writing this, God reminded me of something more wondrous than Woolworth's. He didn't rebuke me for dreaming or thinking about stuff. God just whispered that "Eye hath not seen, nor ear heard, neither have entered into the heart of man, the things which God hath prepared for them that love him" (1 Cor. 2:9 KJV). Sort of sets me to dreaming all over again.

# Marriage in the Morning

ome mornings are better than others. Breakfast devotions were a bit of a downer today since Jud chose to read Proverbs 31 "at" me. Jud beat me (keep reading please) to the shower, coffee, and cereal then smiled and slid "the virtuous woman rises before dawn, prepares breakfast for her family and plans the day's work" down my uncoffeed throat. I fumbled for one of those psalms on the godly man, but without my glasses I couldn't even find a Bible. I made notes to tell Heather and Matt about this marital Maalox moment.

Yes, our Heather's getting married. His name is Matthew Willis. On May twenty-ninth, halfway up a Washington mountain, Matt asked Heather to marry him. Depending on the mountain's height, that could've perched them somewhere close to cloud nine, unlike this morning, which struggles toward cloud four and a half or so.

Matt loves music, mountain climbing, exploring new places, and cycling. I only made the mistake once of introducing him as a biker. They met in college, both concerned with international health issues, both pre-med. One and a half years later they met again in Seattle at an Episcopal church. We've come to believe that God showed up.

Jud likes Matt, which is no small matter for the father of the bride. We rented the video and watched Jud identifying with Steve Martin having his own Maalox moments as *The Father of the Bride*. The wedding's set for December twenty-ninth. That's less than twenty weeks. I'm having a Baptist ball (fun slightly limited by background), and Jud's seeking federal funding.

I'm warning our friends and family that if Jud asks for wedding tips, he's not seeking suggestions. Nor was I, when Jud decided to update me this morning on the attributes of this virtuous woman while I swallowed shredded wheat. Some mornings are better than others, but I wouldn't want to miss a one of them at this place we love to call home.

# Green and Growing

nce a month I write a column for *The Inside News*, a publication for the faculty and staff of Gordon College, the place I love to call home. Recently, Ron Mahurin, an avid golfer, challenged me to write something about this game. Remembering that ignorance of a subject never deterred me before, I accepted Ron's direction for my next piece. While I knew little about the game, even I knew that "There is a green hill far away" did not refer to Augusta, Georgia.

While my Dad, a brother, Uncle Howie, several cousins, nephews, and Chad love golf, I only caught on to the miniature kind. For several of Chad's birthdays and often on family vacations, miniature golf got thumbs up for party time. We'd practice at Vic's behind The Sylvan Street Grille so we'd be "pros" when we took on the cousins in North Carolina. I like a game where the toughest challenge is choosing the color of your ball.

One July when Heather was in California, Chad was twelve, and I was adventuresome, Chad talked me into a game of grown-up golf. The course belonged to King College in Bristol, Tennessee. Jud belonged in meetings at that college, so Chad and I took off to play golf. He was nearing that age when soon he'd publicly deny that he ever knew me. So I felt a game of golf a small price to pay for points I might stockpile as a hedge against that day.

We looked good, an unwritten rule of golf, walking toward the course. Chad toted my dad's old clubs, newly given by Papa to his eldest grandson. I did my part with new white pants and nearly new green-and-white striped knit top. The stripes went up and down instead of wrapping around making me appear larger than life. Never-worn white sandals completed the outfit. I was ready to make some memories.

As we descended the steep grassy slope leading down to the golf course, my slick shoes took me for a ride. I landed on my handicap, looking up at some birdies. Chad, sensitive son, empathized by doubling over, laughing, and rolling down the hill. Cautiously I rose, holding my sandals, scanning to see if anyone had seen my slide from grace. Seeing no one but the hyena at the bottom of the hill, I dug in my heels and inched down to level ground where a twelve-year-old grin with golf clubs stood waiting. When I read Psalm 92 about the righteous staying "fresh and green," nothing holy comes to mind.

First swings impressed Chad and surprised me. There's a difference between beginner's luck and divine intervention. I felt buoyed that God showed up for golf. This was feeling like holy ground until it turned shaky. I stepped onto the green to putt with a wood. What did I know! I just reached in and grabbed the cleanest looking handle. Chad's laughter shook the countryside. I felt like singing, "There's no hiding place down here" or "This world is not my home, I'm just a passing through."

We spent the better part of that summer day playing and laughing ourselves young. We drove, chipped, trapped, and putted through sand, grass, woods, and water. Chad shone and I stunk, but we played our hearts full. No photographers followed. No roped off areas kept fans at bay. There was only one fan, and she had a green handicap.

Several summers have passed since then. Chad and I never played another game of grown-up golf. He grew up and got good enough to play with Mark Stevick and Brendan LeBlanc. They probably even keep score.

We never kept score, but the day's recorded. I'll never sport a green jacket like Tiger Woods, but I've got some white pants with a green handicap, a champion of a son, and a smile-long memory of the day we played grown-up golf.

*the welcome song*

# Phffftness

wo days ago I dragged my body to the Bennett Center and dared it once more to get fit. This was no happy occasion. Travel and company scratched the previous five days of workouts, so I approached the phffftness center with some guilt and fear. The only thing ready about me was my sweatsuit. I'd washed it the night before.

As I lumbered up the stairs to the track, I harbored momentary regrets at having gone public with my phffftness plan. I'd heard somewhere that working out was supposed to reduce stress. Pressure, that's what I felt today, phffftness pressure. My exercise began with hand-pulls up the staircase. Weak knees showcased my heretofore unnoticed upper body strength. Arriving at the top, winded but aware, I listened for cheers. Hearing nothing but breathing—mine—I began my second exercise. Suck in stomach, pinch buttocks together, roll back shoulders, and raise chin. Now, walk past the Nautilus/weight room. If it weren't for fake phffftness, I'd have none at all.

It was close to four o'clock, and my mental list nagged that most of today would show up on tomorrow's list. The only difference between this day and previous years was that now exercise appeared on the list. The sign on the track reminded me that this was an odd day, no argument there. Odd-numbered days meant that one walked or jogged counterclockwise. I could do that. After a few feeble attempts at stretching, I began my trek through the wilderness. No other trekkers emerged on the elevated track above the field house.

My sneakers thudded the padded track as duty pulled me, like a balky toddler, 'round the oval. I knew that my body was the temple of God's Spirit, but today it felt more like a warehouse. Then, something wondrous slipped in, soft, yet stronger than the sounds of my footfalls and breathing. Prayer. Not mine, though I usually did that on days when I walked alone. I craned my neck to see the source of these sounds.

The Gordon College women's volleyball team sat in a circle on the court floor below me. I couldn't make out the words but caught the Spirit. My pace quickened, legs reaching, arms punching air. Then music floated up and lifted me as only truth can. "Jesus, Lamb of God, worthy is Your name. You are my strength when I am weak. You are the treasure that I seek. You are my all in all."

"Yes!" I shouted, then joined their song. "When I fall down, You pick me up," and "Lord, to give up I'd be a fool. You are my all in all." I didn't expect God to show up, especially not in a volleyball uniform. But He did, and He will, in you and me and for us in this place I love to call home and in the place you call home. Phew!

# Wedding Toasts

$M$other and Dad Carlberg celebrated their sixtieth wedding anniversary in October of 1997. Our daughter Heather marries in a few weeks. Both deserve celebrations, but I must admit a particular fascination with eighty-five-year-old lovers since I plan to be one.

I've been a part of the Carlberg clan for most of my life and treasure my Naomi and Elimelech. They spur me to be "more Ruth than ruthless," as Dean Richard Farmer once preached. Dad's a tough old Swede with a booming preacher voice. Behind his back we call him "Big Bob the Baptist." My English mother-in-love's remained gracious. She was a gourmet cook, no small task on a preacher's budget. But a few years ago Mother began forgetting more than what's considered normal, so Dad took to remembering extra and overseeing much of the cooking. Mother recalls what was, so Dad focuses on today and tomorrow. They're still a team.

Last month Mother and Dad stayed with their daughter, Beth, and her family, just down the road in Hamilton. The day before they were to leave for Florida, Beth noticed Mother toasting a fair amount of bread. When questioned, Mom replied, "I'm toasting it to make sandwiches for Dad and me to take in the car tomorrow." Beth protested such dry sandwiches, but Mom ended the debate with, "But Dad loves his bread toasted."

Later on Beth found Dad in the living room and asked when he started preferring toasted bread. Dad said, "I don't like my bread toasted." The logical followed. "Well, Mother thinks you prefer it that way, so she's toasting up a stack in the kitchen. You need to tell her you want your bread plain." Tears watered his tired eyes. "Mother gets notions in her head, Beth. She's convinced that I like my bread toasted. I wouldn't hurt her by insisting on plain bread. What's a little toast between us?"

Most weddings have some kind of toasts for the young lovers, the newlyweds. But before Heather walks down the aisle with her dad, I'll encourage her to spot those two experienced lovers, the 1 Corinthians 13 variety. They'll be seated near the front of the chapel so they can hear and watch their eldest granddaughter marry Matt.

If Heather and Matt are wise, they'll pay close attention to those seasoned lovers, still holding hands and toasting each other after sixty years of marriage. And you can bet God, the Source of Love, will show up to cheer on both old and young lovers. It wouldn't surprise me if Mom, fresh from a morning of "toasting" Dad, might just slip her hand out of Dad's to brush a crumb from the corner of his smile. So, what's a little toast between family and friends at this place we love to call home?

# Sit Close

*M*ost November days in New England frost more than pumpkins. Jud and I huddled close together as we trekked across the frozen grass, exhaling our breath like white puffs into the chilled air. Walking's healthy for the body, but this one brought healing to my soul.

As we walked past the overgrown part of our frozen garden, a memory surfaced. Unearthed from the depths of the heart, like buried treasure. Two holly bushes triggered the recall. They'd been given to me by the college faculty and staff to plant in memory of my dad. He loved gardens and holly, so it was a perfect gift.

We moved into Wilson House, the president's home at Gordon College, just about three years and three months ago and brought the holly bushes with us. The first year I thought they'd gone on to join Daddy. I left them alone for the second year and tossed them a glance now and then until yesterday when Jud and I went outside to check the progress on some renovation work being done on our college home.

One bush sat red-berried as Christmas, and the other sported a fresh crop of leaves. With no one but Jud in hearing range, I cheered and thanked them for surviving, thriving, and daring to reproduce outside our bedroom window. It did me good that they'd made it from the safe world of some greenhouse to Martel Road, our previous home, and now to Wilson House. Sitting close helped.

Several years ago, the chill and the circumstances of the early November day caused Mama, Jud, and I to huddle. We supported Mama between us as we walked from Daddy's graveside service to our car. Jud opened the front door, and I nudged Mama forward with, "Why don't you sit up front with Jud?" She turned and cupped my face in her well-used hands, drawing my eyes to hers. Mama spoke words that change the listener. "Janice, life is short. Never miss a chance to sit close. You sit up front with Jud."

Mama's right. Life is short. She'd said something like that before. But like an outdated vaccine, it never took until God carried Daddy to heaven in the early hours of October 31, 1991. I'd have preferred Easter to Halloween. It seemed like a joke. But then, Daddy loved to tease and stayed a kid at heart, so maybe Halloween was more appropriate than it felt at the time.

We don't have much say about the length of our days, but "sitting close" is ours to choose. My grandma called

*the welcome song*

those decisions "simple but not easy." These truths surfaced today from the place where unforgettables live—the heart.

That's why I love those holly bushes, visual reminders of the value of sitting close through one more winter. It's worth a try. But don't be surprised if God reproduces through you fruit, red-berried and green, resembling the hope and joy of Christmas and Easter. It's for His glory and for the encouragement of any of you who struggle to make the first move closer at the place you call home. Like Mama said, "Life's short. Never miss a chance to sit close."

# Let There Be Light

ights lift my spirit, especially in winter. That's partly why I called on the "elves" from Physical Plant to add some lights to the grounds of Wilson House one Christmas. One phone call to Mark Stowell, and Brian and Jim showed up prepared to electrify the place (and me). I stood ready with hundreds of lights and ideas about how the tree should be trimmed.

The tree grew outside in a small plot of ground highly visible from our bedroom, living room, front entry hall, and across the fields by a few Hull Street residents. This tree could not be lassoed with lights. It needed expert electrical weavers assisted by a woman with the gift of advice.

Brian and Jim swallowed smiles while they listened to me describe how I wanted the lights . . . "wispy-like." So there would be no confusion, I dangled my arms to demonstrate. They acted like this was a normal part of their day. Rain drizzled on their sainted heads while I directed from inside the entry hall. Before long the tree glistened with lights wrapped around the trunk and cascading "wispy-like" from every branch. I couldn't hold back and exuded, "That's the most beautiful tree I've ever seen!" My kids say that I've said that for as many Christmases as they can remember. But I had never said it about an *outside* tree before.

Brian and Jim looked wet but pleased. I think God showed up through them. How else could you explain their attitudes? They decided to add lights around the front door and around the signpost that identifies this place I love to call home. The trustees, cabinet, and their spouses were coming for a Christmas party the next night. Thanks to Brian and Jim, we were lit and ready.

When Tim Stebbings, vice president for finance, arrived at the party, I whisked him over to the window to see the tree "his" men had festooned with tiny lights. Tim smiled like the Grinch and said, "Do you know how many work orders didn't get filled because you wanted a 'wispy' tree?" Actually, I had no clue and felt like covering my ears, just in case he said some huge number. He continued, "There are students groping around in the dark trying to study for finals without the aid of light." I was beginning to feel like a war criminal until I took another look at the tree. It stood shimmering and tossing its wispy-twinkled branches like a long-haired girl in springtime. *A fit of flair shouldn't be terminal*, I thought.

Well, I won't be a repeat offender, at least not on that tree. I promised Brian and Jim that I'd leave the lights strung till next Christmas and hope for a slow growth cycle. Every now and then I plan to flip that switch and set that tree to shimmering, all "wispy-like"—a few sparkles to break up winter. Besides, a little pizazz never hurts. I learned that a couple of weeks ago from someone's old aunt Agnes. She tossed her head and pronounced, "I may be getting older and losing a little of my mind, but I don't plan on losing any of my pizazz."

Me either, Agnes, nor my gift of advice. Essentials at this place I love to call home.

*Part 3*

A Place to Grow

# The Welcome Song

One day, while visiting my mom, I asked, "Mama, do you know this room is cluttered with welcome signs?" She knew. But cluttered? Never! The kitchen eating area and welcomes belonged together like warm cookies and cold milk. I continued, "But the new wallpaper border doesn't go with the colors on that heart-shaped welcome sign." Mama bounced back with, "So when do colors determine welcomes?" This was beginning to sound like conversations between my mother and her mother.

As a child in Chicago, I remember singing a little song in Sunday school—"There's a welcome here, a welcome here. There's a Christian welcome here." We belted it out on cue from our teacher whenever somebody new came to class. I don't think we'd have thought it up on our own. I really don't know how it made anybody feel since it never got sung to me. My daddy was the preacher, so we were supposed to feel welcomed already. It didn't always work that way.

When I was ten years old, we headed for Georgia. Daddy, a Baptist minister, had heard the whisper of God and moved us from Illinois to Georgia. Folks didn't sing that song there to me or anyone else. It's not that they weren't welcoming. It's just that they didn't know the song. They needed somebody to teach them. That was Daddy's job. Through sermons and rolled-up-sleeves kind of work, Mama and Daddy taught and lived the welcome song.

"General welcomes are easy to say or sing," Mama'd say while we worked side by side in her tiny kitchen. Most folks would've had legitimate reasons for not welcoming any newcomers to such cramped quarters. But someone, a stranger turned friend, stitched a sampler to underscore Mama's philosophy. It read, "Small houses filled with love have elastic walls."

Mama and her walls knew how to stretch. And Mama knew how to teach while I reached to peel another potato. "The welcome song's easy to sing when you're singing to your own kind, Janice. But Jesus had something bigger and better in mind. He wants us to learn a few more verses."

The older I got, the more verses Mama and Jesus made me learn. When I was little and sang, "Jesus loves the little children; all the children of the world," the only black baby I knew, even in Chicago, was the doll my parents had given me one Christmas. So I practiced loving "all the children of the world" on one black doll. It took lots more years to know some red or yellow or black children by name. That made it easier to understand why they were "precious in His sight."

When we moved south in the 1950s, we didn't know how threatening the welcome song could be, but Mama refused to stop singing it. "Welcomes come in all colors, Janice."

My color was okay, sort of a basic slightly freckled whitish pink. But I talked funny. I spoke "Yankee," and they talked "Southern." So I suppose if they'd known the song back then, they'd have sung me a qualified welcome. My friends and neighbors came in varying shades of freckled, white, or olive too, except in summer when we, as teens especially, worked at tanning our hides, inching toward the color that would have been most unwelcome by too many.

A few years and lessons later I learned that the problem grew in people not locations. North, South, East, or West had its own way of choosing whom to exclude from the Christian welcome song. "That's the heart of the problem," Mama'd say. "Singing the Christian part of the welcome. Jesus won't let you limit the song to your few favorites."

Peter, one of the twelve disciples handpicked by Jesus, knew the song, at least the general welcome part like most of us are comfortable singing. He was doing just great till God taught him the Christian welcome verse through a vision. Daddy and Mama taught me about it from the Bible so God didn't have to use such drastic measures. The story's found in Acts 10 and 11. Peter was hungry, not for words but for regular food. He'd been praying for a long time, and while he waited for his hosts to prepare the food, he fell asleep. I can identify.

Sometimes when I'm praying, I fall asleep, but I wake up from drooling not visions. Maybe God said something like, "Peter, let me teach you another verse to your welcome song." Then God taught Peter that what He has made kosher stays kosher. And Peter learned that the Christian welcome verse was not just for Jews but for everyone. The Good News of Jesus, the forgiveness of sins, the gifts of the Holy Spirit are for everyone. Then Peter sang his heart out or, more accurately, sang out the heart of His God.

I don't know if they still teach that welcome song in Sunday school, but Mama's still teaching it 'round her table and through her letters and stories. Her kitchen with five welcomes on one wall says a lot about her. But the way she lives that Christian part of the welcome speaks wondrously of her God who loves to teach us to sing another verse.

# Sunshine

few days ago, Jud, Mark Sargent, provost at Gordon College, and I drove to Melrose to attend the memorial service for Marion Wilson, the mother of Dr. Marvin Wilson, a professor at Gordon College. It was one more "to do" on a list too long for one day until God showed up in Melrose to celebrate Marion's life of almost one hundred years. She had always said she wanted to be one hundred but headed for heaven eleven days short of her birthday. A few days before she died, Marion said, "I guess I don't want to be one hundred. I just want to be with Jesus."

Family and friends knew Marion's love for Jesus and for them, and so they gathered to celebrate her loving, long life. And for no earthly reason, God chose to show up and speak and sing through old and young people clustered together to peek at the wonder and mystery of life and death. Marv Wilson spoke first, though he said nothing from the podium. He simply sat on the front row with his wife, Polly, and their grandson, Ian. I watched Ian nestle under the wings of Marv and Polly. Sometimes Ian's head rested on his grandpa's shoulder. And God spoke to me of safe places and strong shoulders and of loving the next generation to Jesus. I want to be that kind of person. I want Gordon College to be that kind of place.

Marv's brother, Malcolm, spoke for the family, sharing wonderful stories. Marv and Malcolm's mother had marked generations through her music, notes of encouragement, poetry, love for Jesus, and memorization of God's Word and hymns. Three great-grandchildren—Ian (9), Jay (8), and Emily (4)—craned their necks and strained their ears to learn how bigger folks live and die. Laughter laced the generations together. Love taught.

As a young teenager, Marion had wondered why so many hungry folks showed up at their doorstep. "We used to call them tramps," said Malcolm. One tramp took Marion outside and showed her the secret. A large X marked one stone by the street, letting all hungry folks know that inside this house was X-tra good food. I want to be that kind of person. I want Gordon College to be that kind of place.

Malcolm announced that his grandson, Jay, would play a number on the cello; then he spontaneously walked over and put his arm around Jay and said, "Grandpa's going to sing along with you." And God showed up to sing and play. Grandpa and grandson took us to the foot of the cross: "Beneath the cross of Jesus I fain would take my stand, The shadow of a mighty Rock within a weary land. . . ." The melody slow and easy enough for a beginning cellist but words tough for even a lifelong pilgrim. But like Polly and Marv with Ian, Malcolm and his wife, Nell, love-linked Jay into a family of Christ followers. I want to be that kind of person. I want Gordon College to be that kind of place. These grandparents pray that, someday, by faith, Ian and Jay will take their own stands beneath the cross of Jesus, and they'll become the strong shoulders, the safe places, the singers, and love-links for another generation.

Today I read about Elizabeth Clephane, the author of "Beneath the Cross of Jesus." She lived for only thirty-nine years, all spent in a village called Melrose in Scotland. Elizabeth was sickly, but her joy was serving others and helping the poor. Her wonderful attitude earned her the nickname "The Sunbeam of Melrose."

I can't imagine a more fitting title for Marion Wilson than "The Sunbeam of Melrose" or Haverhill or Andover or wherever God grew her. Nor can I imagine this place I love to call home without the sunshine of Dr. Marv Wilson—God's strong shoulders, a safe place, and love-link to hundreds of students. I want to be that kind of person. I want Gordon College always to be that kind of place.

Sunshine

91

# Holy Sit-Ups

Across the fields from my living room sits the Bennett Athletic and Recreation Center. No, it doesn't sit; it stands like a massive rebuke to my unhealthy lifestyle. I tolerated and endured the months of ground shaking, dust flying, and noise polluting. When the construction ended, I celebrated that Gordon College had such a state-of-the-art facility for our students, faculty, and staff. I hid behind my tight schedule and resisted eye contact with that holy health site. All was well, except me, until God showed up.

In late July God sat by me in Colorado and gave me courage to take long looks in and around me. August found me practicing deep knee bends on behalf of my suffering sisters and brothers at Gordon. Before I could claim an allergy to exercise, the health site opened its doors. But open doors, free memberships, and Nautilus giveaways could never have lured me from my couch.

Heading to the psalms for comfort one day, I read, "He knows when I sit and when I rise." I never knew sit-ups were biblical. A slow dawning suggested there was too much of a gap between my sittings and risings to be called exercise.

Then last week Jessica and Vanessa, sophomores at Gordon, asked if I'd mentor them. I agreed. Over the weekend, while I was speaking in the Midwest, God showed up in sweats. Not like some thick-necked body-builder but like the maker of muscle, the builder of brain, the creator of cartilage. God came through encouragement to consider physical health as a holy discipline. He came through courage from two sophomores to invite me to be their mentor and wisdom for me to ask them to walk and talk and keep me accountable.

So today we start walking. The Bennett building's built. My temple restoration's just beginning. I'm scared and excited, more hopeful than hopeless. But thankful to be surrounded by witnesses and encouragers to keep me on track at this place I love to call home.

# Stop, Look, and Listen

ast weekend found me racing from United Airlines terminal B to terminal C at Chicago's O'Hare International Airport. I never liked that name *terminal*, though I do understand it. The terminals connect through a tunnel festooned with neon lights above and moving sidewalks underfoot. There's still enough kid in me to love the lights.

A recorded voice pecks away at silence reminding standees or walkers about the rules and limits of this mechanical mover. If you stand, stay to the right. Walkers and runners keep left. There are other options. Elevators lift and lower at the far end of the tunnel. Efficient, but you miss the lights. It's not just that I love the lights; I need them. They, not the moving sidewalk, lead me through that tunnel.

This time, as I descend the steep escalator into the tunnel, I stand a step away from a father and his young son. The lights catch the son. "Wow!" he exclaims. The span of smooth marble between the escalator's last step and the beginning of the moving sidewalk affords enough time for an important decision. I hear the dad say, "Let's just stand and look at the lights." An oddly wonderful sight, father and son holding hands, standing still, off to the side, in the middle of the madness of walkers and racers on mechanical movers. The hurried and hassled check watches, pass slow folks, and race to terminals. They "win" the race but miss the party.

Today, my list lures me into the left lane. Peeks into December set my engine racing. There are other options. A couple of thousand years ago, there was enough kid left in some shepherds to let them see the Light. They stopped, looked up, and held onto their Father's hand. And God led that ragtag bunch of "losers" into the middle of a miracle.

I believe there's still enough kid in you and me to choose the better option this Christmas season. There are exits off moving sidewalks and passing lanes. We can choose to stop and stand, even to kneel for a closer look at the Light. And who knows, God may surprise us with lights in our tunnels and some kind of party. Miracles aren't just for 34th Street. They can happen in the place we love to call home.

# Uncle Faithful

*T*he jewelry box opened with a spring, and before me lay Uncle Jack's valuables, some would say. He died less than a month ago, just missing a chance to celebrate his ninetieth birthday with the rest of us. Maybe that spurred him on to heaven—the thought of one more gathering in the garage.

Uncle Jack preferred the formal dining room, which was never that formal. But Mama preferred the garage, which had never seen a car, for big parties, especially ones with lots of kids and messes. So we followed Mama to the garage for most of our big family parties like graduations, birthdays, and shrimp-a-roos.

A shrimp-a-roo is to this part of the coastal south what a clambake is to New Englanders. It's corn on the cob, salad, watermelon, corn bread, fresh boiled shrimp with cocktail sauce, already sweetened iced tea, fresh churned ice cream (usually vanilla), and a whole lot of talking and laughing. Uncle Jack, like

Daddy, wasn't especially fond of the smell and mess of shrimp-a-roos.

Uncle Jack's our family's bachelor. Until recently I thought he wanted it that way. But not long before he died, he told his nephew, "Don't be a bachelor. It gets too lonely." That's a major confession without a booth, priest, or minister in sight. He lived about five minutes away from Mama in a nicer part of town with one more bath and two more bedrooms than Mama and Daddy had until they put on an addition.

Whenever I came down from north of Boston where I've lived for more than twenty years, I'd make a pilgrimage to Uncle Jack's house to check his garden and his most recent batch of photographs. These were his true treasures. He loved his vegetable garden, flowers, and pictures of family, friends, and missionaries. Most pictures weren't in albums but in baskets on the coffee table. Too many, however, got framed and landed on the fireplace mantel. I say too many not because some weren't worth a glance but because they looked uncomfortable overlapping each other like a gathered crowd going nowhere. With a long look, though, you could see a few generations of family history perched above the fireplace that never saw a fire.

After Daddy died, Uncle Jack took to checking up on Mama. He was Daddy's eldest brother, and he loved my mama, so it was a natural thing to do. Almost every morning he'd come propped up by his papa's cane and with an appetite for one or more of Mama's Norwegian pancakes. He often brought cream for her coffee plus some strong opinions.

"Margaret, you work too hard!" he'd tell her.

Margaret's my mama's name, and hard work's her fitness plan, so this was not some fresh revelation from God.

"Jack, would you like another pancake?" she'd ask politely.

Of course, he did. While he ate, Mama would wash dishes, put in a load of laundry, and feed the dog.

"Margaret, don't you ever sit down?" Uncle Jack would ask. "You're going to kill yourself, and then what will your family do without you?"

Mama's never been one to shy away from challenges, so she didn't sit, almost like she was pushing God to choose who he wanted first, Uncle Jack or her. Well, God picked Uncle Jack.

I miss him. Our favorite thing was holding hands as we walked from his car to the house or the reverse. Sometimes he told me secrets. Since Mama's known for her speaking more than listening, he had some words stored up that needed an audience. I was *it* on occasion. His hands were big and soft like my daddy's, and he sported a massive turquoise and silver ring, the kind that could do damage. But Uncle Jack wasn't into fighting. He loved to read and play the piano, tend his gardens and pray for his family.

Prayer was his primary work, I think, after he retired from Reynolds Aluminum in Arkansas and moved to Wilmington, North Carolina. We counted on those prayers since Uncle Jack didn't do just the general kind like "God bless the Jensen family." He called us by name, like God does, all of us: brothers, sisters, nieces, nephews, spouses, grandnieces and nephews, missionaries, and more. That's work, and it was daily—harder than anything Reynolds Aluminum had tossed his way.

Uncle Jack belonged to the Assembly of God Church in Wilmington. Nobody in the family knew how much his church family loved him until God took him to heaven. It was the younger ones, college age and down, who loved him most. That's why we chose not to fill the funeral home with flowers but gave money to the church for the youth ministries instead. They were also *his* kids, and it was fitting that they called him "Uncle." He listened mostly and saved his opinions for his family. The church members did their best at caring for him as he grew older. "Uncle Jack," they'd say, "we've saved the handicapped spot so you can park up close to the church." But he refused and parked with the younger folks, informing them, "I'm old, not handicapped."

Seems like he got old overnight. His skin stayed soft and young, but he got bent over sometime between last summer and this and took to using his papa's cane to compensate for knees with rusty hinges. And he'd often say to me, "Janice, I hate it when I can't remember names and such."

Me too.

I know lots of people younger than Uncle Jack who can't remember things like saying please and thank you. They forget to write or call or fill a gas tank. Some forget vows and promises and paying bills on time. Uncle Jack only forgot lesser things like a few names and dates. But he never forgot your birthday. The long list hung over his desk like some sacred mandate. It was. He was sort of the official harbinger of the day we were born. No card from Uncle Jack? Must not be my birthday.

Mama worried about him, especially this last year. He fell a few times at home and got dressed for Sunday church on a Friday. The church part's understandable. He loved his church, and they loved him right back. His pastor said, "Jack never missed a chance to encourage me. Told me he wished every day were Sunday."

At his memorial service young people stood to tell stories about their "Uncle Jack." They were his family too. Churches are supposed to be family-like where bachelors and single moms, orphans and widows feel at home. Uncle Jack belonged.

Sometimes I think Uncle Jack should've been a weatherman. I never knew anyone more fascinated by winds, rains, lightning, clouds, and heavens. He read about the planets and stars. When storms came he perched himself on the porch to applaud God's power and wonder over nature. My uncle makes me think of Job, in the Old Testament part of the Bible, except he never really suffered like Job. But then, what do I really know about anyone else's suffering.

It's the part in Job 38 and 39 where God gives Job some clues about who He is through descriptions about His power over nature and all creation. That's the part that makes me think of Uncle Jack, those images of weather: "What is the way to the abode of light? And where does darkness reside? . . . Have you entered the storehouses of the snow? . . . What is the way to the place where the lightning is dispersed or the place where the east winds are scattered over the earth? . . . From whose womb comes the ice? Who gives birth to the frost from the heavens when the waters become as hard as stone, when the surface of the deep is frozen? . . . Can you bring forth the constellations in their seasons or lead out the Bear with its cubs? . . . Do you send the lightning bolts on their way? Do they report to you?"

Uncle Jack read his Bible, but he also took time to sit and wonder about what he read and the God who spoke it all into being. When storms came he didn't turn on his TV. He watched the heavens and cheered the God who controlled it all. Maybe that's part of why he loved church so much. It felt good to gather with people who knew The Weathermaker.

I didn't really want anything out of Uncle Jack's jewelry box. The stuff didn't matter to him, so why should it matter to me? But I changed my mind when I saw the pin with the add-on pieces, like the pins heroes in the armed forces wear. Only he wasn't a soldier or a hero, as far as any of us knew.

It was a Sunday school pin with hooked-on pieces that added up to seven years of perfect attendance. I don't know what seven years they were. He'd attended perfectly as far as I knew. Maybe the church couldn't afford to give him pins for all the years he'd been faithful.

I don't plan on wearing the pin. But I think I'll tack it over my desk as a reminder to be faithful in little things. Seemingly small matters like showing up on Sundays with peppermints in my pockets for the kids and encouragement for the pastor. Like refusing to park in the handicapped spots when I'm not. A reminder to tend to something as small as cream for Mama's coffee or as big as a birthday or as important as being on time.

Maybe Uncle Jack's pin will remind me to grow vegetables, mostly to give away, and to take time to watch God stir up a storm. Or to remember to be faithful in seemingly small matters like driving the same car for more than twenty years so money isn't wasted on things that rust. And mostly I need that pin to remind me that the greater work is faithfully praying name by name for each person in our big family until I can't do it anymore or until God takes me home—so I don't have to celebrate one more birthday in the garage.

# Run with Me

e sat clumped like flower folks transplanted to the backyard of Wilson House. The menu reported that sundaes on Tuesday night were all that remained of our annual faculty/staff picnic. But picnics are more than food. That's why this is my favorite faculty/staff event. For a few hours we're not divided by regalia or roles, titles or job descriptions. We speak family and friends, act sister and brother. It's a good way to begin any worthy endeavor but especially for kicking off a school year at this place I love to call home.

This year the children taught the lessons. We hadn't planned it that way; Someone else did. All we planned was an Olympic theme. John Williams's "Olympic Fanfare" set the stage, and most ceased hugging and talking to watch the far side of the field where someone ran with a stick of fire. It was a child. Halfway 'round the field, children strained or fidgeted for their turn at bearing this Olympic torch. As the torch passed from child to child, none dropped out; all kept running 'til a clump of kids showed up to hand the torch to Jud so the games could officially begin. The torch? A citronella candle wedged inside a tall bamboo holder. The game? A race.

The clumps of flower folks cheered the children as they lined up to begin their quest for an Olympic medal. I'd inched closer to the children so I could snap a photo or two when I overheard this truth: "Please run." Two little girls, probably around five or six years old, sat huddled on the sidelines, one coaxing the other to enter the race: "I promise you. All you have to do is run, and you'll get a medal. I heard 'em say it. Just run." The crowded medal stand proved the tiny teacher right. Everyone received a prize just for running the race.

We older ones know a lot about "the race." We know autobiographies of great runners. We know our own "heartbreak" hills. And some days it's tough to get up a crawl. Sometimes running the race looks like getting out of bed to face the duties of the day. Some days the race is going for chemo, making a tough decision, cleaning a closet, or saying, "I'm sorry."

Refuse the safety of the sidelines. The tiny teacher spoke truth: "Just run." Someone greater than she promised a prize at the finish line to all faithful runners. But unlike Atlanta, our chances of finishing this race increase if we'll clump together and speak sister and brother at Gordon College or at the place you love to call home.

# V.I.P.s Only

The other day I took off for a quick trip to the mall. My day demanded quick or extra quick. I found myself doing something my kids make fun of, but since I was alone I went ahead and prayed for a parking place. I pled, "Not just any slot in the lot of the Northshore Mall but one close to the main door."

To my astonishment, several spots sat vacant beside the handicapped slots. As I whipped into the nearest one, I noticed a small sign marked "V.I.P. Parking Only." Then I noticed there were many "V.I.P."s. When did some parking mastermind concoct this fresh way to send me to the boonies? I steamed into reverse and prowled the aisles seeking something within a fifteen-minute walk of the front door. As much as I needed to obey my fit daughter, who urged me to park far away and walk just for the health of it, this was not the day. Hurry today. Health tomorrow.

As I huffed through the main doors, a smiling welcome-woman forced a pamphlet into my white-knuckled fist. Since when do we need greeters at the mall? Is this turning into some kind of church or religion? Hurried but curious, I walked and read. The brochure invited me to become a V.I.P. shopper. If I used their V.I.P. credit card and shopped 'til I dropped, I would be rewarded with a V.I.P. parking space.

So that's who's robbed me of any possibility of a miracle at the mall! I sped through the three stores connected with my errands. Then I spent the next fifteen minutes walking to my car. I steamed all the way home as the concept of rewarding frequent shoppers worked its way through my mind and emotions. Jud needed to know of this marketing scheme and parking scam. I planned to tell him at supper.

By supper I'd thought better of it. Jud only goes to the mall under great duress. He never equates fun with shopping or "just looking." I'm the happy wanderer. Jud's the hunter. I like looking, touching, wishing, and dreaming. Jud stalks, sights, kills, and walks out. Which is why I decided not to tell him about parking for V.I.P.s only. He thinks I qualify.

I think he doesn't realize how much I save him. Clipping coupons, checking newspapers for sales, and stopping at outlets add up to some serious discounts. Some men don't get it. Sue Wood told me something about her husband, Dr. Ted Wood. He teaches in the economics/business department at Gordon College. Sue said, "Ted, under duress, and I went to the mall. We parted so he could tend to his errands and I to mine. A couple of hours later I returned to see him well rested on a bench. I ached from toting so many packages but felt buoyed by the bargains I'd snatched. I flashed a conquering smile and recounted for Ted all I'd saved. Ted turned teacher on me and said, 'Sue, let me pass on a basic financial principle. You *save* in banks. You *spend* in malls.'" Oversimplification, I'd say! Wait 'til their underwear splits and they have to pay full price!

While simmering over the mall's marketeers, I unloaded groceries and stuff I'd purchased. It took me three trips to empty the trunk of our car. After climbing up or lumbering down a flight of stairs six times and depositing perishables into refrigerator or freezer, I slumped into a stuffed chair with a glass of iced tea and a bad attitude.

With the second sip of tea, an image shifted my focus from malls to Mama at age eighteen. No photos brought this to mind, simply word pictures. She'd gone to nurses training with all her material wealth in one suitbox. Not a suitcase or trunk, a suitbox, tied together so her underwear, nightgown, and a few other possessions wouldn't show up on a sidewalk or in the streetcar.

Mama told how she walked into her dormitory room and found extravagant wealth: two chests of drawers, two beds, two chairs, two desks, two closets. Such luxury for her and Hertha, her roommate. As the eldest of seven, Mama'd known making do more than buying new, and sharing more than possessing. She and two of her sisters slept in one bed, shared one drawer each in the old chest. Now she had five drawers all to herself. Mama remembered how carefully she untied that suit-box and placed the entire contents easily into one drawer. Feeling self-conscious, she took half out and spread the contents into the second drawer. Three remained empty. Mama surveyed her surroundings and felt rich. Backing away from the chest, Mama said, "I wondered if I would ever have enough in my lifetime to fill all five drawers of a chest."

I found myself wondering how many chests, closets, basements, and attics you needed to fill to get to park up close at the mall. While I puzzled, God reminded me about a woman in Proverbs 31. The only line He spoke to me was simply, "Her husband can safely trust her." No finger wagging, no sermons, no guilt. Just simple truth.

Oh, well, a little extra walking might just do me some good.

# Dust to Dust

*A*ll I'd intended to do was dust a little. Very little. The bedroom shelves, painted white, forgive a lot. Dabbing at the dust on the tops of some books set me coughing. I've never found comfort in the notion of people going back to dust. Nor in ministers sifting dirt through their fingers above some casket, reminding graveside family and friends that "all are of the dust and all turn to dust again." I don't like to see it, and I especially don't want to *be* it.

Growing up in a Scandinavian home gave me an extra aversion to dust. Nobody wrote their names on Mama's furniture. If anybody coughed in our home, they were either sick or allergic to the oil we used for greasing furniture. Mama called it polishing. At age four, I became old enough to crawl with purpose. Clutching a well-oiled piece of Mama's threadbare underwear, I scurried under the big walnut dining table to shine all the legs on Saturday mornings. Chairs came next. Any leg that didn't move got oiled.

Saturdays stood for something. It never occurred to anyone in our home that this was "their" day. Sometimes Mama, like her mama before her, said that the only reason for Saturday was to get ready for Sunday. The house, freshly scrubbed, sparkled by noon. Mama's best tablecloth and dishes sat ready for Sunday dinner. Loaves of freshly baked whole wheat bread cooled on the kitchen table. The only other counter space came from the large porcelain drain boards on either side of Mama's sink. She called it her "Youngstown."

Daddy polished his sermon and our shoes on Saturdays. He lined them up so no one wasted time searching on Sunday mornings. Daddy only wanted to seek and find lost souls. Offering money tied inside hankies sat with our Bibles. Sunday could've snuck up as early as eight o'clock on a Saturday evening and we'd have been ready. Those Saturdays flowed with familiar duties, leaving us somehow refreshed at soul level by bedtime. There is rest in ritual.

Dust swatting stirs up more than a coughing fit. Memories of the place I used to call home come alongside this place I now call home—a place full of computers and calendars, dusty legs and scheduled Saturdays. My kitchen's full of countertops, but no freshly baked bread sits cooling. *I'm* trying to cool down though while thinking of errands, projects, phone calls, correspondence, and tonight's menu. Guests are coming for dinner and least of my concerns is crawling under some table to polish a few dusty legs.

Rearranging. That's what I think I'm really doing, just rearranging the dust while I work my mind over with lists and memories. Second shelf, right side reveals a half-hidden treasure, a Bible I stopped using years ago in favor of a newer translation. Daddy and Mother gave it to me for my eighteenth birthday, not long after high school graduation. The dust and musty smell disturb me. Furniture dust, understandable. Bible dust, unthinkable for a Baptist preacher's kid. The brown leather, my choice, since somebody told me when I was sixteen that I looked good in brown. These were the days before women and men got "colored" to know which hues helped them look their best.

My name shines in gold leaf on the brown leather cover. Daddy'd underscored my name again on the inside front cover with indelible ink from his Parker fountain pen: "To Janice Dawn Jensen on your 18th birthday. Love you precious daughter. Mother and Daddy." Then he wrote what he believed with all his heart. "I the LORD have called thee in righteousness, and will hold thine hand, and will keep thee . . . for I have redeemed thee, I have called thee by thy name; thou art mine" (Isa. 42:6 and 43:1 KJV).

Maybe that's why Daddy wrote my full name twice on this Bible. Since God called me by name, Daddy figured he'd better do the same. After all, that's why we used Saturday to get ready for Sunday. Making Sunday special was God's idea, not Mama's or Daddy's. They just took their cues from God.

Makes me wonder when the typical Sundays of my childhood—church followed by Sunday dinner and more church—took such a bad turn in most folks' eyes. Maybe it started to look like work when Saturday started to look like fun. Maybe when Saturday stopped being the day to get ready for Sunday, Sunday became the day to jump-start Monday.

Lots of Saturdays and Sundays have come and gone since Daddy wrote in my brown leather Bible and even more since I crawled under the dining room table to shine some dusty legs. I've learned to adjust to some dust and to reconsider the gains and losses of progress. It's been a long time since Saturday's highest purpose stood for getting ready for Sunday at this place I love to call home.

I'm not sure what to do about it. Maybe tomorrow I'll start by finding an old pair of underwear, globbing some furniture polish on them, and crawling under the dining room table to shine up some dusty legs. It will be Saturday again. And like Scrooge, waking up from his dreams to discover he hadn't missed Christmas after all, I'll have another chance. I could use some ritual—a Sabbath and the pleasure of God's company—before I become the very substance I'm trying to clean off my bedroom shelves.

*Part*

# A Place of Truth

# No Smell of Smoke

*L*ast night a large group of Asian students and some faculty affiliated with Gordon's East/West Institute squeezed onto our sun porch for dessert and dialogue. Before the evening ended, the names of two of our faculty, Dr. Bert Hodges, professor of psychology, and Professor Bruce Herman, chairman of the art department, surfaced in several private conversations. They've marked this place I love to call home and neighboring communities through their faith.

Not for a second would I liken the death of Sarah, Bert's wife, to the loss of Bruce and Meg's house and material possessions. To do that would be as foolish as suggesting that Princess Diana and Mother Teresa were equally great humanitarians. Diana touched some in her limited time. Mother Teresa gave the time of her life. One touched some of society's outcasts; the other lived among the poor and dying, year after year, loving and touching them like they were Jesus. But both women marked this world; which takes me back to Bert and Bruce.

Tragedies and calamities force us to consider life at soul level. Our culture encourages accumulation. Most of us don't deal well with death or loss. But these soul-shaking times act like a bugle call, assembling crowds of witnesses to see if our faith is for real.

Last Saturday Bruce and Meg's house burned to the ground. Friends and curious folks gathered to watch the fire and the Hermans. Some folks puzzled over Meg and Bruce, who held hands and watched their house and the stuff of their life burn to a charred heap. Standing, watching, clinging together's not unlike some folks without faith. But hearing them speak of the mercies of God in the midst of the fire, took faith and grabbed the attention of sideliners. So did standing up in church the next morning, in borrowed clothes, testifying to God's goodness and love. Wide-eyed and red-eyed brothers and sisters heard them proclaim that their true home could never be touched by fire. And some dared sniff the air but found "no smell of fire."

Last June, family and friends, Christian brothers and sisters, neighbors and colleagues drew hope, like breath, from watching Bert lift his head and sing at Sarah's funeral. We marvelled at the risen Christ in their children, Sasha and Joshua, empowering them to participate in the service honoring the God who made and loved their mother. People came to honor Sarah, to show

*116*

love and support for Bert and his children. But we also came to watch and sniff the air for the smell of fire. None.

In the weeks prior to Sarah's death from pancreatic cancer, community happened. Word leaked out about round-the-clock loving taking place on the fifth floor of Beverly Hospital. It preached to balconies, back rows, deepest pits, and sidelines. Eventually, it circled back to campus this fall. And last night one petite Asian student testified to the faith of her professor, Dr. Hodges.

She told Jud, "I majored in psychology and Bible, not too practical, some say. 'What job will you get?' others ask. I've been blessed to have Professor Hodges as my teacher and friend. He makes me ask hard questions, even when I don't want to ask them. He knows about the integration of faith with life and learning. It's in his life, so it comes out in his class. I can't imagine studying psychology in a secular college without the guidance of such a good man."

We watch good men and women of faith. We take courage from their faith in life's fiery furnace. They're not unlike Shadrach, Meshach, and Abednego, except that we know them. Which makes their example teach to our core values. We've sniffed the air about them, like astonished Babylonians, and find "no smell of fire" (Dan. 3:26–27). There is an air about them though. It bears the sweet fragrance of Jesus and helps us breathe better and trust more and practice thankfulness and a deeper kind of loving at whatever place we love to call home.

# Garden School

The young boy swung one leg like a pendulum from his perch on the split rail fence. While he chatted and quizzed, the old woman focused her eyes on weeds. "Wow! That's a neat garden," he remarked. "You do this by yourself?" "Mostly," she muttered, eyes still at ground level. The lad, perhaps used to being ignored, carried on tenaciously. Increasing volume added a hint of authority to his eight or nine years of life experiences. The seasoned gardener weeded while the boy watched.

We were on vacation when I happened on this scene. The garden bloomed in an out-of-the-usual plot on the main street of a bustling town. Most shops rely on signs, lights, or both to lure shoppers to their goods. This store's owner had planted a garden to beckon walkers to inch closer to see the wares. No grand picture windows showcased goods. The garden, like a living Monet, drew you to a simple standstill. Once stopped, you could see some pretty stuff peeking out through the open front door. The front porch and garden seemed to beckon you inside. Like inside was supposed to be even better.

It wasn't. Not that the stuff wasn't pretty or unusual. Some of it I could picture in our home. But the prices said "no" or "not today." I gave every nook and cranny my best gawks and lingers. Nothing "to die for," as some say of the stuff of shops. So I retreated to the front porch where the boy continued to pelt the gardener with words.

"I like all the colors." At this, the wise weeder straightened her back, rested her hands and chin on the hoe handle, smiled, and held him with her eyes. That's when I sensed the presence of God. He looked out through her eyes and hooked one small bit of a boy.

"You like my garden, son?"

"Yup. It's real pretty. Is it a lot of work?"

"Yes, I have to keep at it some every day or the weeds take over. Do you have a garden?"

"Nope. But if I did, I'd have one like this."

"Thank you. That's nice to hear."

The woman pushed back some sweat and a few stray hairs with the back of her hand, then went back to studying her new friend. She must've been almost ten times his age. He, eight or nine, dressed like a GAP kid. She, probably eighty or so, wearing an old dress and socks rolled down to the tops of her muddied Keds. His hair peeking out from a brand-new baseball cap. Hers, gray and pulled back into a soft knot, loosened by repeated stooping and straightening to weed and watch her precious plants. No makeup or gloves protected her from sun or soil. She seemed one with the plants she tended.

Since they'd connected, he talked less and watched more. After a long look he asked, "How long did it take you to make such a pretty garden?"

Watching his inquisitive face, she smiled and said, "This one took me about eighteen years."

"Wow!"

The boy now knew two important facts. One, good gardens take a long time, and two, she had more than one garden.

The boy grew still. Eighteen years is something he'd never experienced himself, much less in relation to a garden. I watched as the old woman looked kindly at his puzzled face. Her eyes seemed to nudge him to believe that he could do great and wondrous things like grow to be eighteen or grow a garden or even more. He steadied his eyes on her, like if he looked long and hard enough he could catch stuff from her he'd never imagined. Stuff better than anything inside the store where his dad shopped.

About then, his dad bounded out the door and down the steps and scooped him off the fence. "We've got to hurry. Your mom and I have a lot we want to do today."

The boy waved to his weathered friend and said, "Thanks. I like you a lot. Someday I'm gonna grow . . ."

But before he finished, his dad pulled him away and down the street.

I followed from a distance but close enough to hear the boy shout, "That gramma lady's not a stranger. She's my friend."

"Can you walk any faster?" muttered the dad.

The young boy, probably used to being ignored, turned up the volume and fairly shouted, "Know what, Daddy? That lady works every day in that garden or it gets full of weeds. Then the flowers can't grow. She works really hard. Eighteen years, she told me. She must really love flowers to spend so much time with them. She likes me too. I could tell. She stopped and looked at me and really listened."

The last words I heard came from his father: "Anybody ever tell you that you talk too much?"

# Georgia on My Mind and Heart

*T*he male side of the Jensen family tends toward restlessness but generally gives God the credit or blame, depending on how life turns out. Erring on the side of God goes over better with Baptists. Standing up in church and testifying to God's leading blesses Baptists more than simply stating that you had an itch to go south.

Before celebrating my eleventh birthday, Daddy'd experienced an overdose of northern, Swedish, and conservative Baptists, so we headed southeast to experience the Southern kind. He credited God with his decision to move us to Marietta, Georgia, and the Sandy Plains Baptist Church. It helped me to believe Daddy felt called by God since I mostly felt scared and curious.

Moving to Marietta taught me more than how to speak southern. Georgia became the place I called home from ages ten to sixteen. Here I first wore high heels (mine not Mama's). At fourteen I sat behind the wheel of Mr. Gann's old Ford and bounced it over red clay rutted fields practicing driving. At Sandy Plains Baptist Church, Joyce and Janet, Reba and Rachel loved a skinny Yankee kid 'til she felt almost southern.

DeKalb, Illinois, to Marietta, Georgia, spanned more than miles. Culture and climate, folks and foods poked at my notions about this country and the church. Collard greens, okra, and fried green tomatoes perked up my view of vegetables. Magnolias grew better than maples. Gnats and jiggers took over for mosquitoes. Tea showed up already sweetened and cold. Church suppers served fresh coconut cakes more often than cherry pies. And heat and humidity could keep you indoors about as much as ice and snow up north.

But something cracked and buckled beneath the red clay soil in this part of the South. A gully of ignorance segregated some folks from others, feeding hate and fear 'til they grew thick as kudzu. Economics, color, education, tradition, and even religion helped gouge this gulf. Here, I first asked Daddy what it meant when a door read "Colored." Public bathrooms and drinking fountains separated "whites" from "coloreds."

To a ten-year-old who "talked funny," a walk around the town square told tales. Men white and colored, in overalls, talked, sat, and spit, but not together. Pickup trucks seemed "white" and Daddy's old Dodge felt "colored." Store-bought clothes looked "white" and the dresses Mama made me out of feed sacks from Mr. Owenby's mill felt "colored." But kids stayed kids, except for talking slower and using words and phrases unfamiliar to one little girl from Illinois.

While I worked at picking up new ways of talking, others strained to catch my clipped speech. One day at recess a group of kids crowded close, begging, "Talk Yankee for us. Y'all talk funny." I figured "y'all" meant my family, so I spoke up like a good Baptist preacher's kid. "Hi, my name's Janice Jensen. We moved here from DeKalb, Illinois. I'm ten and in the fifth grade." They giggled, pointed, and said, "How da y'all say Maretter up 'ere where ya come from?" I puzzled, "Maretter?" They answered, "Maretter! The town where you come to." "Oh! We'd say Mary-etta."

Church changed too. Not the loving part at first, but the sounds and sights of it all. Sandy Plains Baptist Church stood out in the country. After Daddy came, we got indoor plumbing and sanded off the tobacco juice spit from the aisles. Sunday meant clean overalls for some and "extry" fancy clothes for others. But mostly it meant seeing my new friends, especially the Freys, the Ganns, the Whites, and Freddy Rogers. They'd taken to us like family.

Which is what church is supposed to be. But somebody forgot to tell some of the folks. So when God

*the welcome song*

started growin' the church and drawin' outsiders into this "family," ignorance took over, toting fear and hate close behind. Some hit us with dreaded names from the fifties like "Communist," "Damn Yankee," and "Nigger lover." Others threatened us and killed our dog. I wondered how they could sing "Amazing Grace" from memory yet never know it by heart.

Daddy never liked confrontation. Me either. So we moved to North Carolina and left "the ministry" and some good friends and hard-workin', struggling folks back in Marietta, Georgia. Daddy didn't want Georgia on his mind or heart or one speck of red clay on his feet. I couldn't forget so easily.

With Daddy out of the preaching business, we acted more like normal folks—scared and curious. Mama made a home in rented space while Daddy worked at selling church bonds to make money and stay loosely connected to the church. I'm not sure if God led or we fled, but even a sixteen-year-old recognized Egypt. Either way, God came along.

Which remains a mystery—a God who shows up and stays. Maybe not as much for the coronation times as for the common and crummy ones. The times when I blamed Him for leading my Dad nowhere. The moment spit slid down my fourteen-year-old leg because somebody blamed me for inevitable change. And the day I sang "Amazing Grace" and recognized how "white" and "colored" my own heart looked. I could've been a Georgia native, singing from memory but not by heart.

Lots of years passed between coming to North Carolina and returning to Georgia. But one day long after Daddy's itch to go south had become an ache in his heart, God put Georgia back on his mind. The Lover and Maker of all kinds and colors of folks led him back to the place I'd called home for almost seven years. Mega-malls and major subdivisions now grew out of my childhood countryside, linking Marietta with Atlanta. Antique and specialty shops ringed the old town square. But best of all, the kids who'd loved me southern stood strong and led in church and community. They'd learned to sing another verse of "Amazing Grace." This time by heart.

The church still lacks color. North, South, East, or West, it doesn't matter. And folks still slip God credit or blame Him for leading them one way or another when it could've been just an itch to move someplace new. Daddy knows better now. He took off for heaven about six years ago and lives with God's family of colored folks—brown, black, yellow, white, or freckled. Best of all, he's met Amazing Grace. Not the author of the hymn, John Newton, but Grace Himself, Jesus the Christ. And don't you know all God's colored folks love singing, "I once was blind but now I see" and knowing it was grace that led us home.

Standing up and testifying in church about God's leading goes over better with Baptists. It sits better than simply stating that you've got an itch to go south. I'm not saying God can't work through an itch. He did.

# Court Appearance

*T*he instructions were simple enough: "Report at 8:00 A.M. for jury duty." Only one problem; "Sit on jury" appeared on none of my lists. However, the thought of a possible $2,000 fine for failing to appear motivated me to get to Salem for my day in court.

Some fifty or so assorted citizens strode, trickled, or slunk into the gathering hall. Court assistants informed us through lectures and videos. One judge joined us briefly to thank us for doing our duty. Then the great wait began while judges determined if they'd need a jury, and lawyers debated which potential jurists could be trusted with their client's verdict. One judge kept mispronouncing the plaintiff's name, finally resorting to spelling.

Jud and Chad had warned me to be prepared, so I arrived with my tote bag full of notes to send, fresh lists to make, and my copy of *No Ordinary Time* to read. But before the work of this day came a quick read from the Psalms, which I carried in my purse for emergencies. Wouldn't you know it, God showed up through my random flip to a passage for some SOS kind of encouragement. I opened the small book to Psalm 96 and read in verse 10, "The LORD reigns. The world is firmly established, it cannot be moved; he will judge the peoples with equity."

I slipped the *New Testament with Psalms* back into my purse. God's words settled into my heart. My God, the Judge of all the earth, not a new thought to me or to you probably. Yet that reminder in the basement of a courthouse with a ragtag bunch of potential jurists served me well. Such a Lover of the likes of us and those who await trials by jury or fire can be trusted with daily dreads, unending lists, and whatever 8:00 A.M. surprises await at the place we call home.

In the final pickings, I didn't end up on any jury. But according to the computer, I served my time and won't be eligible for recall for three more years. That's good news. The best news, however, came through the psalmist, a reminder that my God is the Judge of all the earth. Just and merciful and full of love for me and you. He knows us and calls us by name, the right name . . . perfectly pronounced.

# Sticker Price

hat a week! I must've hurt my neck while craning it to dodge the Wenham police. The problem wasn't speed. My expired sticker caused the pain. I felt obviously guilty with my wrong-colored "3" glaring from the right-hand corner of my windshield. Jud and I'd been travelling so much that April kind of surprised me. April meant a "4." I knew that, so I tried to slink into the nearest gas station, hoping the police would not show up. Richdales, like most convenience stores, don't do stickers. A station in Gloucester did, so I slipped in with a "Whew!"

The fifteen-dollar inspection fee seemed cheap for so much absolution. I felt almost sixteen again, eager to show all I knew about cars. Experience confidently switched signals, honked horns, slammed emergency brakes, and beamed lights while my clean engine purred. After 120,000 miles this machine knew better than to pollute in public. But still I was thrilled when the mechanic reached in and scraped off that 3. While I adjusted the mirror to untangle the hair I'd twisted into a snarl, he made his move and slapped that new sticker in place.

This was no ordinary 4. Instead, a white square with red letters spit "rejected" onto my windshield. I took it personally. Judging by the mechanic's smile, so did he. Courage surfaced and I asked, "Why?" He grinned, "Too much play." Now I'm an eldest child and have rarely been accused of "too much play." Defensively I fought back with, "Is evaluating the driver a usual practice for this GAS station?" I pressed my case in his face: "Isn't this a car inspection?" His lips slid into a crack in his face. Then, as a final insult, he floated some papers onto my front seat, found his lips, and sneered, "You have twenty days." *Who does he think he is*, I snorted. *Some doctor?* I counted to four and showed him my reverse.

As I left the station I caught him in my mirror. He was doubled over by the Coke machine, like someone in pain. With one hand he held his stomach and with the other he motioned someone to come to his aid. When I last looked there were two others trying to make him feel better by laughing. *Laughter's good*, I thought. *I could use a little, just for the health of it.* Maybe with some distance I can find some humor in this humiliation. Meanwhile, I think I'd better take the back roads to the place I used to love to call home.

# Just One Tiny Dash

*M*ama called this morning full of stories. Words like "God's goodness and grace" or "I'm so thankful" or "best retreat ever" come easily to her. Mama's not shy when it comes to talking about God or slinging adjectives. Since Daddy died, I usually get the early edition of Mama's travels. I don't mind. I need practice, since listening's a family weakness.

She and her sister, Joyce, loved Branson, Missouri, and a week at Stonecroft, speaking for a Christian Women's Club conference. Sounded like all those shows and concerts did them as much good as a revival. After a while, I interrupted to give my ears a rest. "Mama, I don't know any other eighty-one-year-old mothers flying all over the world, stockpiling frequent flier points to share with their kids and grandkids."

She responded predictably, "Isn't God good!"

That's how most of our talks end, on a God note. Then we hung up so Mama could dash off to the grocery store to pick up some bananas, coffee, half and half cream, and a few staples. She'll be smiling and talking to herself up and down the aisles about the goodness of God. I know her.

Inexperienced ears may think her trite. Of course God is good when times are good. I admit that phrase wouldn't mean as much to me if I hadn't watched Mama exclaim it also in the toughest of situations. She used it during radiation treatments, working double shifts as a nurse, or dealing with difficult times in our family. When finances dictated squash casseroles night after night, God was still good. Though some family or friends disappointed or dropped her like a plague, God stayed good. Even after Daddy died and Mama found herself alone in a king-size bed after fifty-three years of marriage, God remained good.

Last week I read a thoughtful article by former president Jimmy Carter. It appeared in *Family Circle*, one of the better magazines at grocery checkout counters. It was entitled "Papa, This Is the Life" (July 15, 1997). The article referred to the contrast between our strivings for grand achievements and the simpler things of life, like time with grandchildren. One of President Carter's grandsons, while fishing with his grandfather exclaimed, "Papa, this is the life."

The article began with a story of the funeral for Mrs. Martin Luther King Sr. and a presentation there by Rev. Otis Moss of Cleveland, Ohio. "Reverend Moss said that there would be a marker on Mrs. King's grave, with her name and a couple of dates—when she was born and when she died—and a little dash in between. After extolling the great life of Mrs. King, he reminded us that everybody has what might be considered just a tiny dash. The question is: What do we do with that little dash, which represents our lives on earth?"

Sometimes when I'm down home in North Carolina, Mama and I drive over to Oleander Gardens where Daddy was buried almost six years ago. It takes us a little while to locate the grave marker since the cemetery has regulated that all monuments be flush with the ground. The small, bronze plaque reads:

Harold Edward Jensen
1912–1991
Margaret Tweten Jensen
1916–
"LORD, thou hast been our dwelling place
in all generations."

—Psalm 90:1

Such a short dash. Daddy didn't do all he wanted to with his; it came and went so fast. But I remember some of his better moments. Daddy dashed off a sandbox for me and my brothers one Saturday. Most preachers would've been too busy thinking about Sunday to tend their kids on a Saturday. He bought the wood early in the week and sanded and painted it; by Saturday he only needed to nail it together and dump in a load of sand. He built it big enough for all our friends (even our neighbor's St. Bernard, Happy). Daddy's gravestone doesn't state, "Built sandbox for his kids and their friends."

From my fifth grade year through most of high school, Daddy dashed from his studies and pastoring to pick me up after band practice. I don't remember him ever being late. He'd be waiting in the car looking like he loved what he did. Like picking up his daughter ranked right up there with preparing sermons and praying for sick people. He never missed a concert or parade either. We never had enough money for many family photos, but my memory's full of snapshots of my dad grinning and cheering me on. The funeral notice didn't mention those times out of his life.

During my growing up years, Daddy had every right, according to our culture, to dash away from the table and listen to the evening news or retreat for some deserved quiet. He chose to stay at the table. Around the dinner table we learned Bible verses, teased, talked of the day's adventures, and read chapters from great books. Sometimes Daddy got as silly as we, doing tricks with his knife and fork or telling jokes. Mealtimes made memories. They're not etched on marble, brass, or newsprint but forever on my heart.

In the middle years when too many of Daddy's dreams died, he dashed off in ways that confused his family and friends. He dishonored his marriage and left "the ministry." Hindsight helps a little but not much. We're all pretty complex people. God knows; I take comfort in that. The genes we inherit and the demons we fight don't catch God off guard.

We're vulnerable to the enemy's tricks when tired, discouraged, or depressed. Dead dreams weigh us down. I felt helpless watching Daddy grow tired, defeated, and distant. Back then, it was more common to tend problems by ignoring them or running away. Daddy did both. He seemed like a beaten wrestler, we a stunned audience.

He grew stronger and healthier in the last quarter of his life through God's grace and Mama's love and forgiveness. He shifted his focus by burying his dead dreams and encouraging Mama and his kids to pursue theirs. He cheered well and we responded. If you liken this dash called life to a race, Daddy sprinted his final laps.

Probably his greatest work took place away from pulpits or hospital rooms. He accumulated little money and not much stuff. Daddy never drove the car of his dreams. But he rallied for the fourth quarter. The last leg of his dash focused on encouraging his children and grandchildren and helping Mama write her books. Daddy arranged her travel so she could dash off to places he'd never dreamed of to speak to numbers he'd never imagined. Some called him a "loser." Losers can't act that big.

Daddy loved his children and grandchildren. After practicing on his children, he perfected grandparenting quickly. To them he was Papa. He watched their games, attended recitals and plays, and took each grandchild out for ice cream or breakfast alone. He showed up on time or early for anything that mattered to them.

Mama's gift was talking, Daddy's was listening. Grandkids loved having Papa's full attention. Something deep and lasting happens when someone loves you enough to really listen eyeball to eyeball. He loved their friends too. Daddy welcomed them, especially in summertime when the beach beckoned. That's why so many kids attended his funeral. He'd used up a good bit of his dash on them. They wouldn't miss this last chance to say, "Thanks, Papa."

Somewhere in the Bible it says, "Don't despise the day of small things." Maybe that means like building sandboxes and showing up on time. It could also mean sitting still, listening to your grandchildren. Or encouraging Mama to write and fly away to speak to thousands while he stayed home and watered the gardens. Daddy's dash is over. A beginning and ending date testifies to that truth on his grave marker.

But just under Daddy's name is Mama's: Margaret Tweten Jensen. The year of her birth, 1916, followed by a dash, awaits a few final numbers. Sometimes I feel strange looking at Mama's name while she stands beside me. I once told her so, and she said, "Me too." We often talk about how short life is, just a tiny dash between birth and death. Next thing you know, we're laughing and talking about the Lord of this dash called life. Before you know it, Mama's exclaiming all over again, "Isn't God good!" Only somebody who really knows Jesus can take a long look at one tiny dash and come away laughing.

God is good and I am grateful. So good that He shows up while I write to remind me of the significance of small things in the Bible: one small stone in a slingshot, a few small dips in the Jordan River for a leprous leader, a little boy's lunch for a multitude, and a faint cry from a criminal on a nearby cross: "Jesus, remember me when you come into your kingdom" (Luke 23:42). Way to redeem your dash and win the race at the buzzer!

# Piano Lessons

ome decisions never made it to a family discussion. Take piano lessons, for example. We took them. My brothers and I used up whatever inheritance we might've had through years of taking non-negotiable piano lessons in the place we didn't always love to call home. Taking lessons differs considerably from studying piano. Usually, the only time I really studied piano took place whenever Mama took a notion to plop herself beside me on the piano bench.

Daddy's method served me better. He'd sit nearby in an overstuffed chair and listen like I was somebody worth hearing. It felt like God showed up. Appreciative audiences, even of one or two, tended to push me over my practice time. Still, often as I raised my rear, ready to run, he'd simply ask, "Do you have an encore, Janice Dawn?" Usually, I'd exhausted my repertoire, so I'd flip back to the beginning of "The Spinning Song," hoping to trick his ears into believing this was worth his time. Daddy taught music appreciation right in our living room. He loved me by listening to nothing much for as long as it took me to play it.

During my twelfth year, some wisdom slipped in between hormones. I caught on that a few changes in practice time could free me from dinner dishes. If I did homework before supper and practiced afterwards, Mama'd be so busy thanking Jesus for my change of attitude, she'd gladly do the dishes without me. This dish dodging did something for my interest in practicing. The more pots, pans, and piles of dirty dishes, the greater my urge to practice. The remains of fried chicken, mashed potatoes with gravy, or rice pudding could keep me at the piano the better part of an hour.

"Gettin' by" disappeared whenever Mama slipped in beside me on that piano bench. She'd studied piano, so she knew how that red John Thompson book was supposed to sound. You couldn't fool her with Bach or any other composers from those yellow Schirmer books, either. She and my teacher believed in scales; I believed they were kid-hating, fun-squelchers.

About the time I'd think I was home free, thundering hoofs headed my way. Next thing I knew, Mama'd be tapping out the beat, slapping her dishpan palm against the top of the piano. She could spank out a rhythm, leaving the piano shaking and me willing to scrub pans, even with rusted scouring pads.

140

My love-hate relationship with piano lessons changed in my thirteenth year. A handsome, talented man became my teacher. Overnight, I stopped taking lessons and began to study piano. No piece too demanding. No practice enough. Mama thought God and I'd finally come to terms. I thought I'd found true love.

It all blew apart later that year during a lesson. I still blame Mama. She'd cooked cabbage the night before. It has a way of taking over my insides, leaving me feeling too full. As I sat at the piano, giving one of my best performances, I could feel the pressure rising. Pinching my buttocks together, I raised myself to new heights in personal piano performance.

The hairs on Mr. Everett's arm brushed mine as he leaned over to turn the page. I think he lingered. Maybe he liked the Evening in Paris perfume I'd splashed on after Mama dropped me off. He nodded approval as I played my heart out. It takes a great deal more concentration than most thirteen-year-olds have to lay yourself out at one level while holding back big time at another.

The piano piece ended with a flourish. Mr. Everett shouted "Bravo!" then slapped me on the back. That move relaxed me just enough to transform me from a piano performer into a wind instrument.

I blame him for that.

The following week I signed up for French horn.

*Part 5*

# A Place to Celebrate

# The Wedding Gown

he wedding dress looks at home in our bedroom. It hangs from the canopy railings atop the bed built by my brother for our twentieth anniversary. My mama first wore this gown almost sixty years ago. I wore it too. Mama let me play house in her wedding dress when I was growing up, especially on stormy days when anything good had to come from inside the house. Mama'd open up her cedar chest and let me pull out some memories. Sometimes we sipped tea and nibbled edges off cookies and picked our pleasures from the Sears catalogue.

The catalogue's history but not my memories or Mama's fifteen-dollar wedding gown. Heather wore it December 29 when she married Matthew. The ivory satin and lace gown's smaller than I remembered, but then I'm much larger than when I first tried on Mama's shoes and gown and pretended to be a bride.

But Heather wasn't pretending when Grammy's gown slid over her as perfectly as the glass slipper over Cinderella's foot. And neither were the generations that squeezed into the first small pew in the chapel of Christ Church. We'd gathered like some "pew" foundation to give away something more valuable than money. Our treasury held commitment, mutual respect, service to God, and His children mixed with a whole lot of good and not-so-good experiences, mistakes, and sins. But over and under all was a commitment to follow Jesus Christ and determination to finish the race together until "death parts us."

Almost 145 years of marriage squeezed into the first pew as five of us took our assigned seats. Mother and Dad Carlberg held hands and the record of more than sixty years of marriage. Next to them sat Mama, holding a damp handkerchief and memories of her wedding gown and marriage to my dad for more than fifty-three years. My daddy probably sat with Matt's mother, Irene, and witnessed this celebration from their heavenly perch. Jud sat low on his thinned wallet, wrapping my hands in his. After thirty-two years of marriage, he knew best how to settle my heart and keep me from fidgeting. I'd already dropped two mints and my gloves.

The wedding's over, but the marriage is just beginning. It may not be a bad idea to keep Mama's wedding gown hanging at the end of the bed or within view.

Storms come. The stinging rain of a serious illness may pelt at your peace. Financial uncertainty can undermine hope like a gully washer. Infertility, miscarriage, or testy toddlers or teens might stretch your patience like a sail in a thirty-knot wind. And questions that nibble at your faith can wrap you in a fog so dense you can't take a step in any direction. There will be days when whatever's gonna be good has to come from inside this place I love to call home.

# Bubbles and Beaches

ast Sunday felt too hot for going to church, even though I'd awakened early enough. Old New England churches, while white steepled and picture perfect, generally aren't air-conditioned. It must've been close to one hundred degrees outside with high humidity that day, so I toyed with the notion of staying home. With our kids in California, I didn't need to fret about being a bad example. Besides, they're old enough that whatever I've been before them is pretty firmly fixed. Furthermore, Jud was in Asia on college business, so I felt as if this day should or could be all mine.

Over coffee, an old idea from my Baptist upbringing slipped in with the newspaper: "Remember the Sabbath." Remembering wasn't my idea. I wanted to forget and get to the beach. "Rabbi Ya-should-a" won, so I dressed lightly and headed for church. Since I considered myself on vacation, I vacated my church and drove to the nearby Hamilton Congregational Church.

The mid-August sun streamed through the stained glass windows, steaming the parishioners. I squeezed into an aisle seat near the rear of the church. Duty kept me smiling, standing, singing, praying safely through all the rituals of playing church until God showed up. O.K. I know God was already there. But I didn't recognize Him.

For me, He showed up during the children's sermon. One of the ministers squatted down kid-sized and began blowing bubbles. Folks on the front rows weren't as amused as the children. "Today, children, we're going to talk about blessings. Did you know that bubbles are a blessing?" They squealed out an assortment of yeses. "Do you know what a blessing is?" Finally, someone said that it was something good. One little kid blurted out, "My birthday's in October." Birthdays are big-time blessings to most kids.

The minister continued, "There are blessings that come and go, like bubbles, and ones that never go away, like God's love." He told them and us to think about the blessings we enjoyed. Then he prayed, "Praise God from whom all blessings flow." Big words and a bigger concept for kids of any age. At his "amen" small folks with one or more of their parents scampered back to sticky pews or children's church. Some took off for the nearest sink to de-bubble themselves.

*Bubbles and Beaches*

That's when I spotted some blessings—Gordon College grads, with babes in arms or kids in tow, heading back to pews or off to children's church. Jud and I've been at Gordon for almost twenty-two years now. Some of those grads would've missed church even on a cool Sunday back in their undergrad years. The bed or beach would've won. But here they were on a sticky Sunday in August shunning the beach and showing up at church, bursting old notions as surely as soap bubbles clapped between a child's hands.

Perhaps God clapped too. Proud Papa surveying his kids growing on, maturing. Imagine those nail-scarred hands coming together, clapping and cheering us on when we make one simple but tough choice. Choices like taking our families to church and staying with them. Choices like putting down the newspaper, getting dressed, and heading for church instead of to a golf course, beach, or air-conditioned mall on a sultry Sunday in August.

After church and lunch, I took a book and beach chair and headed to Good Harbor Beach to enjoy some blessings. There was a time in my growing up years when that would've been perceived as "sinful." Sipping iced tea and drinking in the salty air left me feeling refreshed, not sinful. Actually, I felt much more comfortable than I had in church. But then, church isn't about my feelings or yours. It's about obedience and thankfulness rooted in love. It's doing what's right even when the heat's cranked up and nobody's looking except the only One who really matters.

Eventually, I left the beach earlier than planned. A boy on the blanket next to me had discovered a jar of bubble water among his playthings. While his mother napped, he squealed and whipped a plastic wand through the air, scattering circles of soap too close for comfort. I laughed and thought, "Been there; done that." Enough "blessings" for one already sticky Sunday. So I folded my chair, swatted a bubble, and headed for the place I love to call home.

⁓

# Philodendron Folks

*M*ama and I sat sipping coffee in the breakfast nook of the place she loves to call home. It's the room with the view. "Look at those philodendrons!" she exclaimed. Mama loves gardening and flowers but favors the easy-care varieties. That's why the hanging baskets grew practical philodendrons this year instead of Boston ferns. I had given her the ferns the year before, sort of a living link between her New England family and the North Carolina ones. Besides, ferns look more southern to me, sort of a soft and flowing kind of pretty.

But Mama can take just so much fussing in plants or people. She gave them her best, but they needed too much tending, so this year she brought in her faithful "phils." "Look at those beautiful plants, Janice. I hardly ever tend them. You'd have to work to kill one." They swung slowly in the soft morning breeze, adding color and life to the porch that "grew" under the garage roof's overhang.

The hangover roof was Daddy's idea. "It won't cost much more and will keep the garage-office cooler and give us a shady place to sit." Daddy was right. The roof was sort of the "faithful phil" of the construction world. It gave a lot for a little.

As I write, Mama's watering her long, leafed friends. "I think they could benefit from a good drink of water this morning." She's holding the green plastic watering can at arm's length over her head looking like some sort of soft sculptured artwork. Problem is Mama's the kind of art that makes you laugh more than think lofty thoughts. The angle's all wrong. She's not tall enough to tip the can and pour into the center of the plant, so she sort of gives it the heave-ho. I watch her shudder as she waters her right armpit and half her dress. The plant's still reeling and thirsty. It looks like Mama and the porch floor got most of the benefit.

I've got some "faithful phil" kinds of friends. My Michigan Marty has never forgotten my birthday, and I've rarely remembered hers. I've never heard her complain. She's never made me feel as if tit for tat was the game we played and I was the loser. That predictable card's become a symbol of friendship. We see each other too seldom for the friendship to have survived. But it does and it will, because Marty Lefever's a "faithful phil."

Then there's Carolyn Wilkie. We grew big bellied together during our baby-making years and love each other's children almost as much as our own. In the years before our personal baby boom we rode together to teach school. Carolyn asked questions to draw me out, to help me know who I was. I didn't always like the questions, but I grew to love Carolyn. Our children call her "Aunt Carolyn." She's earned that title by being a "faithful phil."

There's a story in the New Testament about a man named Barnabas. It says in Acts 11:24 that "he was a good man, full of the Holy Spirit and faith." Everybody's full of something; Barnabas was full of the Holy Spirit. Your chances increase greatly of being faithful at anything when you're full of God. I can't explain how or why God does this, but some mystery is good for us. When Barnabas came around it was like God showing up to encourage you. His name means encourager. "Faithful phils" are like that. They don't suck the life out of you with their neediness. They're too busy filling your tank.

Mama's a sight this morning in her turquoise mumu and red plaid slippers. Her beautiful white hair and wondrous face look odd perched on top of that costume; it's like mixing Easter and Halloween. To add to the look, the tag of the mumu sticks up the back of her neck like a small flag, telling the world the size, fiber content, and brand name. I said something to her this morning about her outfit. "Mama, there comes a point where parents

are a reflection on their children. That time is now."
Mama laughed. "I love this mumu. It's perfect after I
shower. Lets me dry naturally."

Well, Mama's got some extra drying out to do today
since she sloshed those hanging baskets with some Norwegian *ufda*. (That's a word that can mean anything
you need.) Her right slipper squished as she headed
toward the back door, empty watering can in hand.

She's a rare one. "Faithful phils" are hard to find too.
Rare ones like Barnabas, Marty, Carolyn, and Mama so
busy watering others that they aren't aware that God
showed up and gave them a drink.

# Dinner on the Grounds

After running around in jeans and clogs for several days, the thought of dressing up brought mixed feelings. Jud and I'd been in Colorado for nine days, most full of meetings connected with Jud's being on the board of the Coalition for Christian Colleges and Universities. A printed sheet told us where to meet and when to eat. We anticipated the three days we'd scheduled as vacation between meetings in Denver and Frisco.

Our conference center condo in Frisco, Colorado, stood alongside a clear creek, across from a range of rocks and evergreens God used to craft and color mountains. The white noise of a rushing stream dulled distractions and freshened my mind to feel comfortable with quiet, more settled in spirit. The dry climate coupled with the sound of a fast flowing creek encouraged me to drink more water. This necessitated more frequent use of the facilities near our bedroom, giving me a limited form of exercise and a feeling of weight loss.

The condo allowed us to "eat in" more than out, something most preachers' kids know well. During my growing up years, eating out meant one of two options: Somebody'd invited us to their house or our church was having a potluck. When I was ten we moved from Illinois to Georgia and much changed about the place I loved to call home. For one thing, church potlucks became "dinner on the grounds."

Several times a year dinner followed Sunday morning services. Food showed up spread across several picnic tables or on planks placed across a couple of saw horses. To my way of thinking, only Scandinavians and southerners excel in this culinary extravaganza. Dinner on the grounds catered to more than our need for food. It served up an extravagant celebration of the joy of belonging somewhere, somehow.

If you happened to just be "visitin'" on that Sunday when dinner showed up, you'd get picked out and rounded up for the party. Lost people seem to show up better in small churches. I don't mean necessarily lost in the theological sense, but more like folks without a home church, or a place to belong. Sometimes they did show up really lost "for all eternity" as Papa used to say. Such lostness gave me shivers.

Good cooks serve up great bait. Mrs. Rogers' fried chicken or Lillie McGinley's fresh coconut cake could hook and reel you in faster than you could say, "Thank you. I'm just looking." Next thing you knew, you'd be bawlin' at the altar or teaching Sunday school. Good cookin' does not encourage neutrality.

Makes me think of Jesus fryin' fish by the lake and askin' Peter a tough question: "Do you love me?" (John 21). Peter'd learned large lessons in the preceding weeks about himself and about this Jesus. The questions hurt yet helped heal Peter's aching heart. Yes, as much as he loved fish and fishing, he knew he loved Jesus more.

Standing around this breakfast fire burned him with the memory of another fire in another place when he'd denied that he even knew this Jesus, much less loved him. And now, fresh from a cross and resurrection, Jesus again reeled Peter close to His side with our church's favorite bait, "dinner on the grounds." Imagine, God Himself, Jesus squatting beside a fire, frying fish, and inviting somebody as lost feeling as Peter to get in line and "come and dine."

Jud and I dressed up last night and headed out for one of those rare but diamond-studded dinners, according to somebody's rating scale. The grounds, green and manicured for golfers, spread like velvet in the valley, making the rocky mountains all the more rugged and majestic by contrast. The restaurant, an old rancher's log cabin, sat awkward in such lush surroundings, sort of lost without tumbleweeds, scrub pines, and wildflowers.

158

Doormen and people with titles I can't spell greeted us and walked us to our table by a window. Pine walls and chandeliers of antlers plus a view of the lake and mountains lured me with their rugged simplicity. After an un-asked-for appetizer, "compliments of the chef," Jud and I laughed at the oddness of two Baptist preachers' kids in such a setting.

We didn't know the chef. Why would he want to bait us with free food and the semblance of a relationship?

We held hands, prayed, and then exclaimed over the works of edible art placed before us—pheasant soup followed by trout and elk set on plates of such decorated splendor it made you want to wait a while and just watch your food. Jud wasn't quite as keen on lingering and looking as I. It was difficult enough to keep him seated after a few bites once he spotted fish jumping in the lake. He'd rather catch them than eat 'em, no matter how fancy you fuss up his plate.

The dinner on those grounds was worth those diamonds or stars or whatever rating system this world chooses to applaud its cooks and planners of culinary celebrations. But I, for one, hope I never get too used to this world's scorecards or grow to think I deserve diamond-studded gourmet dinners set on manicured grounds. I was made to enjoy "dinner on the grounds" and to make lost folks find their place at the table. 'Cause someday Jesus is gonna ring some kind of dinner bell, and family I never knew from every tribe and nation will gather for suppertime in a place He calls heaven. And we won't even be able to count the diamonds or imagine what will come our way, "compliments of The Chef."

# Postponed Party

*A* winter storm pelted the party out of our Christmas this year. The month of December usually tilts toward overload, so Jud's decision to cancel the faculty/staff Christmas party didn't strike me as an act of the Grinch or Scrooge. I needed a few free hours at home more than I needed a party. So, last December I thanked God and Jud for the gift of one snowy night at the place I love to call home.

In March, however, I needed a party more than a few free hours at home. March madness affects more than basketball lovers. And blizzards aren't the only storms capable of kicking the party out of life. So I showed up with a new haircut and a hankering to "let the games begin."

Our food service presented a feast for sight and taste. They made Martha Stewart look like a mudpie maker. Jackie Meers, Jud's administrative assistant, and I'd planned the "One Starry Night" party back in November, expecting to make December sparkle. But God knew the dullness of March needed the boost of a star-spangled celebration. We scattered stars over tabletops, onto programs and napkins. Only the March sky showed up in clouds.

I've grown to expect clouds more than stars in March. They'd rolled in on me throughout most of the winter. I needed the hope of a party. The day of the party one call followed another from Mama in North Carolina: "Doctors found cancer in Aunt Jeanelle this morning," and "Lena's had a stroke. Please pray." I'd been praying and hoping. Sometimes it's better to party.

It takes faith to party. To feast and sing and celebrate shakes a fist of faith at the enemy of our souls. And we do have an enemy who slithers and slinks and steals our joy. I couldn't find my joy until I dressed for the party. Sometimes joy hides in the dark of duty. And joy multiplied when I saw faculty and staff and recalled many stories of courage and faithfulness to serve God in the dark where we shine like stars.

Today I read Exodus 20:21: "The people remained at a distance, while Moses approached the thick darkness where God was." I prefer light, so I tend to distance myself from the dark when I have the choice. Sometimes I'm afraid God won't be in the darkness I face. But I take courage in the image of Moses approaching the darkness.

*162*

Jackie and I didn't discuss theology when we planned "One Starry Night" last fall. We just wanted a party with a simple theme. God knew the storms ahead, so He gave us three gifts. He sent one snowy night with a few free hours in December, then a party in March when we needed a touch of Christmas, and our friend and staff member, Carol Bussell, who reminded us in the middle of her storm against cancer, to trust God in the darkness. Our great and faithful God is there *and* here in this place I love to call home.

# Mama's Fitness Plan

*M*ama called this morning, just to check in. She usually leaves me feeling winded. Not because of overtalking but from overlistening. Focusing full attention on someone else takes more out of me than I usually have to give before eight in the morning. Hearing about her yesterday and her plans for this day leave me slightly spent.

Mama's eighty-one and can pack more into a day than three forty-year-olds. She'd leave Martha Stewart breathless and guilt-ridden. Before she called to tell me about her plans for the day, she'd already done what I'd call a couple of days' work out in the garden. I'm sweatin' just picturing her combing that dirt, pinching dead buds while bending over like a model for those yard cutouts with polka-dot bloomers.

Mama weeds like a bent-down machine, defying unwanted growth to take root among her prized periwinkles and dozens of other flowering plants. Her gardening outfit affects property values. She struts forth in a uniform of paint-speckled polyester shorts, a clashing sleeveless blouse, Daddy's old socks rolled down into worn, muddied sneakers, topped off by her shower cap. Imagine all that classic white hair wound into a beautiful French twist and tucked under a pink plastic shower hat! If laughter's good for your health, she's kept several neighbors around longer than their genetic makeup or life expectancy charts suggested.

A couple of months ago, Mama and I were speaking in Canada. They put us up in one of those hotels with glass elevators. A health/exercise area surrounded the base of the elevator. This meant that elevator rides tended to make you feel motivated or guilty since you could watch folks stretch, pedal, row, climb, and twist while you rode up or down in air-conditioned comfort. Mama felt neither.

One morning as we descended to the level of fitness, I could feel Mama's dander rising. She began to shake her pretty white head and glare down at a wide array of men and women twisting and shouting their way through their morning locomotions. Suddenly, Mama exploded her philosophy of fitness to any within earshot, "Do your own yards!"

A few seconds later, the elevator opened and we threaded our way through the svelte and smelt, heading toward breakfast. Once seated, I cautioned, "Mama, you've gotta be careful not to talk so loudly. What if one of those fitness folks had heard you?" Mama never missed a chance to teach or preach. "Maybe there'd be some more pretty gardens and a few more families working together. Why, can you imagine my mama and papa hanging around a gym in spandex with towels around their necks?"

Coffee exploded from my mouth. Mama and I laughed 'til our eggs grew cold. Then she continued. "Mama did her bending and stretching while scrubbing her red linoleum in the kitchen. Papa walked almost everywhere. He never owned a car. To them, 'gym' was a young man who lived down the street." This time our howls brought glares from two tables and our waitress. I spurted out, "But they would have called him 'Yim.'"

At this the waitress brought our check, and we hurried to the rest room to doctor our faces and salvage our pride. We were to be picked up in ten minutes to be driven to One Hundred Huntley Street for an interview on their television program. I wondered if they were adequately prepared for Mama's spontaneity and her philosophy of fitness.

I reminded her of our Canadian caper this morning when she called. Her laugh erupted as I described a long line of Norwegian relatives trying to grasp the concept of climbing steps that go nowhere or rowing machines without fish for reward. "And to think they call this progress! What's happened to all the time these work-saving devices were supposed to hand us? Seems to me most folks I meet seem pretty harried, often needing the gift of a few more hours for each day." I looked at the stack of correspondence and junk mail on my counter and mumbled, "You're talking to one of 'em, Mama."

She left me laughing and rethinking her philosophy of work and health. Mama could talk for just so long. Work called. She needed to finish watering before the sun baked everything. I could picture her grabbing hold of that water hose like it's some kind of balky reptile and whipping it around the yard like a seasoned snake handler. Work never drove her. She pushed it out in front of her where she managed best. Don't bother hanging around to hear her complain. She's nothing but thankful.

Ever since Daddy died, Mama's been saving up for an underground sprinkler system. She could've had three or four by now. Whatever's been saved, she's given away several times to grandchildren, her church, Gordon College, or anyone else in need. Next to needy folks, sprinkler systems can't get off the ground or under it. So Mama spends the better part of her early mornings hosing down her acre of grass and gardens, hanging baskets, and two birdbaths.

Anything that grows seems better off when she's around. Birds freshen up in her yard. Grandkids swarm through her back door. I'll bet even Jehovah's Witnesses and Mormon missionaries feel pretty good around her, even though she is a Baptist-Presbyterian. When you're really thirsty, most folks, fowl, or flowers don't care if water comes from a hose or a goblet.

That's why I can't help but laugh at the thought of her, a muddied and determined old gardener. Combing those rows like a treasure hunter. Giving the neighbors their daily hoot with her outlandish outfits. Strutting forth like the general of gardens, barking orders at weeds and flowers. No sweet-talk. And they pretty much obey. It wouldn't surprise me at all if God showed up to sit a spell on her porch swing to watch one of His children do her morning devotions. Bending, kneeling, and lifting holy hands and a pink-shower-capped head in thankfulness to Him who thought up gardens and the gardener and called 'em both "good"!

# Blessings

*M*arch madness for Mom and me didn't include three-pointers from mid-court. We were making points from podiums and pressing to match up our weary bodies against a tough schedule. No visible scoreboards kept track of our wins or losses. One banner flagged the contest: "Living the Legacy." Women of all ages seemed eager to grab pointers from two older players who longed to bless their generations and those who followed with true riches. The kind Jesus talks about.

After the last retreat concluded, I flew to North Carolina to enjoy a week with Mama. This trip home combined business and pleasure. I'd have the pleasure of my mother's company, and we'd do the business of deciding which child or grandchild should get "this or that" from her small stock of treasures. I valued time with Mama, not the business of being reminded of the brevity of life. But like a "good" eldest child, I pressed on to do what was expected.

What followed was an illustrative teaching from Matthew's Gospel on the limitations of "treasures on earth." Mom had precious few, but the stories surrounding them increased the value of each tiny treasure. I marvelled at her detachment from the stuff of life and her eagerness to "bless someone" with a book, bureau, or some bit of herself.

It wasn't like she was dying or anything. At least not any more than any of the rest of us. Mom just wanted to make sure she'd passed on something special to each one of her kids and grandkids, some legacy or inheritance. Psalm 61:5 reminds me of the legacy Mom lives: "You have given me the heritage of those who fear Your name."

Our culture's big on names. We name-drop, call each other names, and shop for name brands. But we're not too good at fearing the name of God. I'm not altogether sure what that means except as I've seen it lived out through Mama in this place she loves to call home.

Somebody who fears God doesn't seem to focus much on things. Mama knows where her true treasure's stashed. It's not in North Carolina, so she's perfectly at ease detaching from this stuff as we amble from room to room. Phones ring and Mama carries on like she has nothing to do but tend the telephone. People who fear God's name seem to do better when interrupted.

God likes Mama's company. He showed up in her laughing eyes and ease with which she talked about matters of life and death without so much as a flinch, cough, or tear. That legacy of faith is the blessing Mama's passed down. She's the treasure. I think that's partly why God likes hanging out with her. She's a good reflection on His name.

Someday, I hope many years from now, her children and grandchildren will come back to this place she's called home. We'll talk of Mama's life and the funeral service. As the eldest, I'll tell them that Mama left something for each of them. Nobody will rush for the stuff. It won't matter as much as staying together. Then we'll start singing. We'll sing songs like "Praise the Name of Jesus" and "Great Is Thy Faithfulness." We'll eat and laugh. We'll cry and hug. Before you know it, we'll be counting our blessings and most will have faces. Then somebody's apt to remember one of Grammy and Papa's favorites and like ribbon 'round a treasure we'll hold hands and sing, "Turn your eyes upon Jesus. Look full in His wonderful face. And the things of earth will grow strangely dim, in the light of His glory and grace." Now that's a blessing!

# The Love Story

ama's writing a love story. She's written before. I don't know how many copies of *First We Have Coffee* came off the press and into the palms of thirsty readers. But these were stories about her Norwegian family and how they learned some of life's valuable lessons. I'm not saying they weren't love stories. They were. But not in the way Mama's writing now. This kind takes fiction.

It piques my interest to picture my white-haired mama hunched over her yellow tablet, writing about lovers. Probably because I grew up in a Baptist preacher's home and assumed I was immaculately conceived. Not that I put myself on a level with Jesus but because I couldn't picture my parents doing what had to be done to make me come about the normal way. I did not suffer from information overload.

The level of my ignorance surfaced one day in my early teens. We lived in Georgia back then, and I rode a bus to school. One morning as I crossed the church parking lot to wait for the bus, a man in a parked car motioned for me to come closer so he could ask me a question. He needed directions. I should've known there was something wrong with him. Most men don't do that.

While I puzzled over how to send him, he suggested that I ride with him. I said, "No, sir. I've got to catch the school bus." He took hold of my arm, smiled sickly, and asked, "Are you a virgin?" My mind raced through its limits. In the heat of the moment, it did the best it could. I pulled free and declared, "No, I'm a Baptist."

He peeled out of that parking lot like he'd connected with some alien. In a way he had. As a kid we sang in church, especially on Sunday nights, "This world is not my home. I'm just a passing through." Passing through on the ignorant side, I'll admit. But you can just hear so many sermons on how "we are not of the world but in the world" or was it "we are of the world but not in it," before you get fairly confused about how or where you really live.

Some of that confusion carried over into the parking lot that morning. That's probably how I came to see Baptists as opposites from virgins. I trace it to my limited knowledge of sex and theology. I knew that Catholics believed in the Virgin Mary. Baptists didn't believe Mary was as important as Catholics did. In the parking lot of a Baptist church I figured this man was testing me to see if I knew my theology. I've since learned that parking lots are fairly good places to check out what folks really believe. Anyway, I let him know I was no Catholic virgin, like Mary. This girl was Baptist.

At supper that night when Daddy asked about my day, I told him and Mama about the man in the parking lot. Daddy was in the middle of some Norwegian meatballs and mashed potatoes when the "virgin Baptist" part hit. His napkin flew to his face, hiding all but his eyebrows. Judging by his forehead, I'm not sure if Daddy was startled or proud. Maybe both.

So you can see why I'm curious about what Mama's writing. Yesterday she read a little to me. Next thing I knew she was telling me some nonfiction about her and Daddy. "Janice, if I had it to do over again, I'd be more passionate with your dad. Life's too short to be so careful and practical with this thing we call love."

It felt a little strange talking to my eighty-one-year-old mother about passion between her and Daddy. But Mama continued, "I grew up Baptist." She didn't need to say anything else. I could fill in the duties. "I knew what was wrong more than right sometimes. Your daddy grew up 'worldly.' He'd done lots of things before he became a Christian (or a Baptist)."

Mama went on to tell about one special Valentine's Day dinner with Daddy. All of us kids were married and gone, and the two lovers were left home alone—one practical, the other more worldly. Mama, the practical lover, set a fancy table for two with candles and a special dinner. She'd baked a heart-shaped cake to top the evening. Baptists generally do well in the food part of love. She'd bought a recording of music from *Dr. Zhivago* and put it on with dessert.

Something happened with the music. While Mama swallowed some cherry heart cake, Daddy rose from his chair. He walked over and reached out his hands to her. Much to her surprise, he asked her to dance. Just like in the movies Mama's never seen. Mama couldn't help thinking Baptist. The Southern branch doesn't dance. But something Song of Solomon-like rose up in her, and she thought to herself, "I'm almost seventy, and I've never danced. That's long enough!"

Daddy never knew the theological battle waged before their waltz. He only felt Mama's love. A love that risked change and restored passion. I wonder if God flipped the record, since it sounds like they danced the night away. Which is what good love's meant to do anyhow. And where better to practice such deep theology or write love stories than at the place we love to call home? Sure beats a church parking lot.

**Jan Carlberg** is welcomed across the nation for her captivating way of telling a good story. Besides being a sought-after speaker, she is the author of *The Hungry Heart*, the wife of Gordon College president Dr. R. Judson Carlberg, and the daughter of best-selling writer Margaret Jensen. At Gordon College, Jan has served as the director of orientation for new students and as the assistant chaplain, and she currently supports its leadership team.

Jan's sensitive heart and love for people fine-tune her knack for gathering a story from the ordinary happenings of life. She loves the ongoing adventure of discovering fresh ways God loves to show up, hallowing the everydays of our lives.